CHRISTMAS
ORNAMENTS
TO
Crochet

Spring House Press, 3613 Brush Hill Court Nashville, TN 37216

ISBN: 978-1-940611-48-8

Printed in the United States of America

First Printing: August 2016

Note: The following list contains names used in *Christmas Ornaments to Crochet* that may be registered with the United States Copyright Office:

6060; American Felt & Craft; Beadsmith; Beadalon; Bead Landing; Cascade Heritage; Clover; Delta Sobo; Etsy; Glass Eyes Online; Fiskars; Hakko; Hobbs Bonded Fibers; Martha Stewart Crafts; mk crochet; Nature's Garden; Plaid; Sculpey; Sulky; Tulip

To learn more about Spring House Press books, or to find a retailer near you, email info@springhousepress.com or visit us at www.springhousepress.com.

PUBLISHER: Paul McGahren

EDITORIAL DIRECTOR: Matthew Teague

EDITOR: Kerri Grzybicki

TECHNICAL EDITOR: Charles Voth

DESIGN: Lindsay Hess

LAYOUT: Ashley Millhouse

PHOTOGRAPHY: Danielle Atkins

PROJECT ILLUSTRATIONS: Megan Kreiner

STITCH & TECHNIQUE ILLUSTRATIONS: Carolyn Mosher

CHRISTMAS

ORNAMENTS

TO
Crochet

31 FESTIVE AND FUN-TO-MAKE DESIGNS FOR A HANDMADE HOLIDAY

BY MEGAN KREINER OF MK CROCHET

SPRING HOUSE PRESS

CONTENTS

INTRODUCTION

There's something magical about decorating a Christmas tree. My kids become giddy with excitement for the holidays when the glow of soft tree lights and the scent of pine fill our home. For me, what makes trimming the tree truly special are the ornaments that carry special meaning for my family. There are ornaments to celebrate our first Christmas together, our first house, and each baby's first Christmas. There are ornaments from trips we've taken, ornaments painted by my kids, and ornaments that belonged to my grandparents. It's like decorating a tree with our most precious memories and happy moments.

When you crochet a project from this book, you are putting your love and creativity into a very special ornament. From tasty holiday treats and adorable woodland friends to a complete nativity set, I hope that you'll find the perfect ornament to gift or to keep and cherish for many Christmases to come.

Merry Crocheting!

Megan Kreiner

TOOLS AND MATERIALS

Since the projects in this book require small amounts of yarn and just a few tools to create, it's best to go with quality over quantity. It's always worth using the best-quality materials for your special projects!

YARN

All of the projects in this book were made using Cascade Heritage 150 sock weight yarn. Please use your favorite brand of sock weight yarn (available online and through your local yarn shop). The yarns used in each project are listed in the resource section (page 133) in the back of this book. If you choose to use yarn of a different weight (such as worsted or chunky) to make toys instead of ornaments, make sure to adjust your hook size accordingly.

STUFFING

Ornaments are stuffed with polyester fiberfill, which is readily available at most craft stores and will maintain its loft over time.

CROCHET HOOKS

Crochet hooks come in a variety of materials, sizes, and handle styles. It's ideal if you can hold and try out a hook or two before purchasing. All of the projects in this book were made on a Clover brand Amour hook, size C (2.75 mm). My personal preference is for hooks with ergonomic handles, especially when working with thinner yarns.

For the most accurate sizing, refer to the millimeter measurements when selecting a hook for your project. You can also refer to the chart on page 131 for crochet hook sizes. If you find that your stitches look too loose as you work, try decreasing your hook size.

NEEDLES

A few steel tapestry needles (size 13 and size 17) are a must for when it's time to assemble your ornaments. Skip the plastic needles as they tend to bend. A size 20 or 22 embroidery or chenille needle is also good for embroidering other details.

In addition to the steel needles, you may also wish to purchase a set of beading needles to apply tiny seed bead details to your completed ornament.

SCISSORS

When working with yarn and felt, a good pair of fabric or sewing scissors will make for clean cuts and quick snips. I also recommend a small pair of cuticle scissors, which can be helpful and more accurate when cutting out small felt shapes like circles.

FELT

Craft felt comes in a variety of colors and fiber contents such as polyester, acrylic, wool, and bamboo. Because the felt pieces for ornaments tend to be rather small, it's worth purchasing good quality felt as well made felt tends to be denser and holds a cleaner edge when cut. When applying felt details to your ornament, I've found that gluing the felt pieces on (and holding them in place with a few marking pins) is often much easier than sewing them in place.

Information about the felts used in this book can be found in the resource section (page 133).

GLUE ON 4 MM PLASTIC EYES WITH LESS MESS! FIRST, DO A DRY FIT FIRST TO GET THE PLACEMENT OF THE EYES JUST RIGHT. PUT A SMALL AMOUNT OF GLUE ON A PIECE OF PAPER. REMOVE ONE EYE AND ROLL THE EYE POST IN THE GLUE. PUSH THE EYE BACK DOWN INTO PLACE AND REPEAT ON THE OTHER EYE.

PLASTIC EYES

Some of the ornaments in this book call for 4 mm plastic eyes. I like to purchase my plastic eyes online because of the variety of options available. Plastic eyes are often available with sew-on loops or fitted with a plastic post that can be coated with craft glue and inserted into the face of your ornament. In addition to plastic eyes, you can also purchase wire glass eyes or glass beads for your project.

In regards to 4 mm safety eyes, I've found that there are subtle variations in the sizing; sew-on 4 mm eyes run a bit small; 4 mm post eyes with no safety backing are in the middle; and 4 mm safety eyes with a safety backing are a bit bigger.

If plastic eyes are not available to you, you can also try applying French knots in black yarn or embroidery floss, small circles of black felt, or even small dabs of black fabric puff paint.

JUMP RINGS

8 mm to 10 mm jump rings are small metal rings in various finishes that can be found in the jewelry making section of your craft store. The rings are sturdy and easy to attach to your finished ornament with just a few stitches.

BEADS

Add a little extra sparkle to an ornament by adding a few tiny seed beads with a beading needle and invisible thread. Larger beads can also be used for berries on holly or to decorate ornament hangers (page 18).

To help keep tiny seed beads organized, try using leftover plastic Easter eggs. It's easy to scoop the beads up off the curved sides of the egg with a beading needle and you can close up the egg to store the beads in a pinch.

For tips on creating personalized beads, check out the ornament hanger customizing section on page 21.

THREAD AND GLUE

To attach seed beads or felt, consider purchasing a spool of "invisible" thread. Invisible thread is a clear plastic filament thread that is clear and is difficult to see. One caveat for the thread is that, because it's clear, it can sometimes be a challenge to work with. I will often put down a piece of white paper and thread a beading needle in front of it so I can see the thread more clearly.

When gluing on felt and plastic eye details, a general craft glue like Sobo Premium Craft & Fabric Glue works very well. Whichever brand craft glue you choose, make sure it dries clear and goes on fairly thick so it doesn't soak into the yarn fibers before it has a chance to dry.

ADD SOME STRENGTH TO YOUR INVISIBLE THREAD BY CUTTING A PIECE TWICE AS LONG AS NEEDED AND FOLDING IT IN HALF. THREAD BOTH ENDS THROUGH YOUR NEEDLE TO CREATE A LARGE LOOP. ONCE YOU'VE DRAWN THE NEEDLE AND DOUBLED UP THREAD THROUGH THE SURFACE OF YOUR WORK, YOU CAN SLIP THE NEEDLE THROUGH THE END OF THE LOOP AND PULL FIRMLY TO SECURE THE THREAD BEFORE YOU START SEWING ON BEADS.

PUFF PAINT AND GLITTER

Ice your gingerbread kids (page 51) or give your ornament a dusting of snow with white puff paint and a dusting of white glitter! Look for fabric paint that is white with a thin applicator tip. Glitter paints tend to dry clear, so look for one that dries white. To give your fabric paint some sparkly, dust the piece with white fine glitter and set aside to set overnight. Shake off the excess glitter once the paint is completely dry.

If you make a mistake with your paint, you can wash it off while the paint is still wet, but let your piece dry completely before trying again.

WIRE AND WIRE TOOLS

Jewelry wire comes in a variety of finishes and can be used for ornament details or for the ornament hangers. A thicker 16 gauge and thinner 20 gauge work well. In addition to the wire, three basic tools are recommended: wire cutters, fine round-nose pliers, and flat (duck bill) pliers.

I found the quality of the wire cutters and pliers improved considerably when I purchased them separately instead of in a jewelry kit. I recommend the Beadsmith and Hakko brands.

For more information on creating ornament hangers, see page 18.

RIBBONS AND TWINE

Ribbon and colorful twine is widely available in craft stores in a variety of colors and sizes. A simple loop is all you need to hang your ornament on a tree!

When tying and applying bows of ribbon to your ornaments, you can keep the cut edges of your ribbons from fraying with a bit of craft glue. Once the bow is tied, cut the ribbon tails ⅛" to ¼" longer than needed and apply a light coating of craft glue to just the underside of the ribbon ends with your finger. Allow glue to dry, then trim through the glue-coated ribbon ends.

NOTIONS AND STORAGE

Here are a few more goodies to add to your ornament-making arsenal!

Stitch counter: A row or stitch counter will help you keep track of where you are in your pattern.

Marking pins: Super-helpful in positioning your pattern pieces before sewing everything together and for holding glued felt in place as it dries.

Split or locking rings: Use these plastic rings to help keep track of the end of your rounds or for when patterns call out for "place markers" (pm) to mark useful landmarks on your work.

Automatic pencil and sticky notes: Great for jotting down notes and sticking them into your book as you work.

Plastic tackle box: Perfect for organizing a bead collection.

Project bags: A small project bag (like a pencil or makeup case) is great for storing smaller tools and notions; a larger bag can hold everything you need for your current project. I find that reusable canvas shopping bags make great project bags!

CROCHET STITCHES

Whether you are brand new to crocheting or are a seasoned pro, this section will provide a complete overview of all the stitches used for the patterns in this book as well as some great tips and tricks on how to get the best results out of your work.

Slipknot

1 Make a loop with a 6" tail. Overlap the loop on top of the working yarn coming out of the skein.

2 Insert your hook into the loop and under the working yarn. Gently pull to tighten the yarn around the hook.

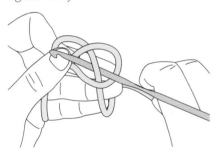

Yarn Over (YO)

Wrap the yarn over your hook from back to front.

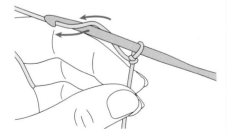

Chain (ch)

1 Make a slipknot on your hook.
2 Yarn over (YO) and draw the yarn through the loop on your hook. You will now have 1 loop on your hook with the slipknot below it.

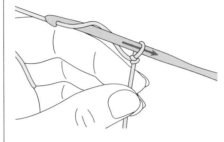

3 Repeat step 2 until you've made the number of chain stitches specified in the pattern. When checking your chain count, remember that only the chains below the loop on the hook should be counted.

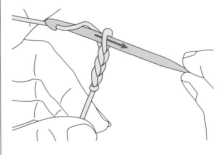

Slip Stitch (sl st)

Insert your hook into the next chain or stitch. Keep your tension as loose as possible, yarn over, and draw the yarn through the stitch and the loop on your hook.

Single Crochet (sc)

1 Insert your hook into the next chain or stitch and yarn over. Pull the yarn through the chain or stitch. You will have 2 loops on your hook.

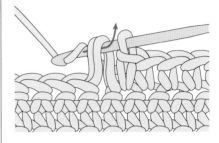

2 Yarn over and pull yarn through both loops on your hook to complete the single crochet.

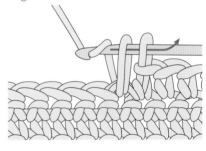

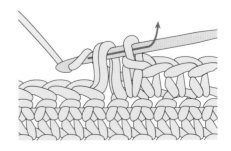

Half Double Crochet (hdc)

1 Yarn over and insert your hook into the next chain or stitch. Yarn over a 2nd time and pull the yarn through the chain or stitch. You will have 3 loops on your hook.

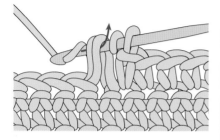

2 Yarn over and pull yarn through all 3 loops on your hook to complete the half double crochet.

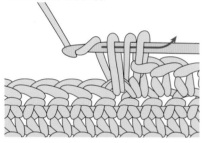

Double Crochet (dc)

1 Yarn over and insert your hook into the next chain or stitch. Yarn over a 2nd time and pull the yarn through the chain or stitch. You will have 3 loops on your hook.

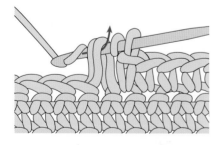

2 YO and pull yarn through just the first 2 loops on your hook. You will have 2 loops remaining on your hook.

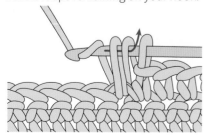

3 Yarn over and pull yarn through the last 2 loops on your hook to complete the double crochet.

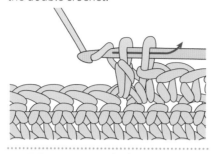

Treble Crochet (tr)

1 Yarn over 2 times and insert your hook into the next chain or stitch. Yarn over a 3rd time and pull the yarn through the chain or stitch. You will have 4 loops on your hook.

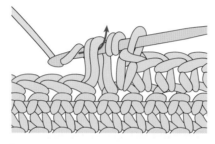

2 Yarn over and pull yarn through the first 2 loops on your hook. You will have 3 loops remaining on your hook.

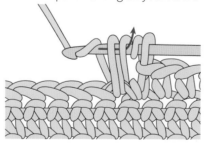

3 Yarn over and pull yarn through the next 2 loops on your hook. You will have 2 loops remaining on your hook.

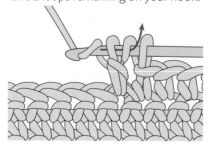

4 Yarn over and pull yarn through the remaining 2 loops on your hook to finish the treble crochet.

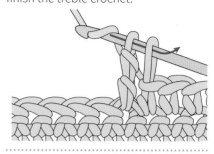

Front Post Single Crochet (FPsc)

1 Insert your hook below your next stitch to the right of the stitch's post. Work the hook around the post from front to back to front again and yarn over.

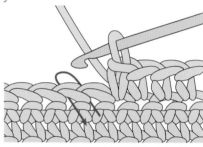

2 Pull the yarn around the back of the post. You will have 2 loops on your hook. Yarn over and pull yarn through both loops on your hook to finish the stitch.

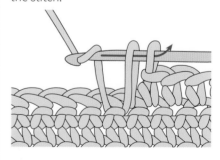

Back Post Single Crochet (BPsc)

1 Starting behind your work, insert your hook below your next stitch to the right of the stitch's post. Work the hook around the post from back to front to back again and yarn over.

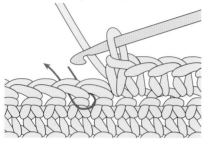

2 Pull the yarn around the front of the post. You will have 2 loops on the hook. Yarn over and pull yarn through both loops on the hook to finish the stitch.

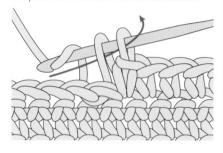

You can also work around the post using other stitches like half double crochet (FPhdc/BPhdc) or double crochet (FPdc/BPdc).

Increases (sc 2 in next st)

Work 2 or more stitches into the same stitch when indicated.

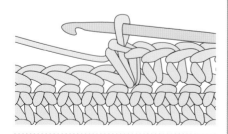

Decreases

There are two kinds of decreases used in this book: skipped stitches (sk) and single-crochet decreases (sc2tog).

Skip (sk)

Per the pattern instructions, count and skip the number of stitches indicated before working the next stitch in the pattern.

Single-Crochet Decrease (sc2tog)

1 Insert your hook into the next stitch, yarn over the hook, and pull through the stitch, leaving a loop on your hook. You'll have 2 loops on your hook.
2 Repeat step 1 in the next stitch. You'll have 3 loops on your hook.
3 Yarn over the hook and pull through all 3 loops. You'll have 1 loop on your hook.

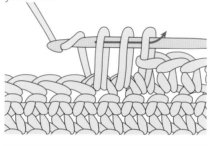

Invisible Single-Crochet Decrease (sc2tog)

This technique can be used instead of the standard single-crochet decrease. It helps eliminate the gaps that can sometimes occur when using the standard single-crochet decrease.
1 Insert your hook into the front loop of the next stitch and then immediately into the front loop of the following stitch. You will have 3 loops on your hook.

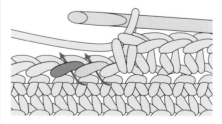

2 Yarn over and draw the working yarn through the 2 front loops on the hook. You'll have 2 loops on your hook.

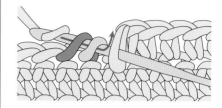

3 Yarn over the hook and pull through both loops on your hook to complete the stitch. You'll have 1 loop on your hook.

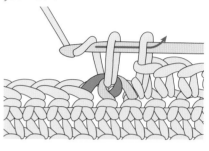

For an invisible half double crochet decrease (hdc2tog), yarn over first and then proceed to decrease as written for the single-crochet decrease until you have 3 loops on your hook. Yarn over and draw through all 3 loops to complete the stitch.

Working in Back Loops (bl), Front Loops (fl), and Both Loops (tbl)

Unless otherwise noted, work in both loops of a stitch except when the pattern instructs that a stitch should be worked in the back loop or front loop. The front loop is the loop closest to you. The back loop is behind the front loop. If a round or row begins with "In bl" or "In fl," work entire round/row in that manner unless you are instructed to switch.

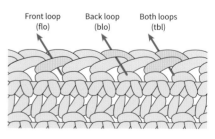

Front loop (flo)   Back loop (blo)   Both loops (tbl)

CROCHET TECHNIQUES

Working in Rows

Work the pattern until you reach the end of your row. Turn your work. Before beginning your next row, you will be asked to make a turning chain per the pattern instructions. Once your chain is completed, insert your hook into the first stitch in your new row and continue working the pattern. It is important to note that you should avoid working any stitches into the turning chain.

Working in the Round

Many patterns in this book are worked in a spiral round in which there are no slip stitches or chains between rounds. When you reach the end of the round, simply continue crocheting into the next. If needed, use a stitch marker to help keep track of where your rounds begin and end.

Adjustable Ring (AR)

The adjustable ring is a great technique that will minimize the hole in the middle of your starting round.
1 Form a ring with your yarn, leaving a 6" tail. Insert the hook into the loop as if you were making a slipknot.

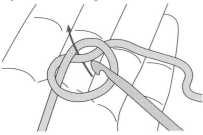

2 Yarn over the hook and pull through the loop to make a slip stitch, but do not tighten the loop.

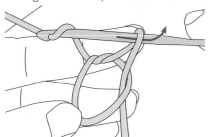

3 Chain 1 and then single crochet over both strands of yarn that make up the edge of the adjustable ring until you've reached the number of stitches indicated in the pattern. To close the center of the ring, pull firmly on the yarn tail.

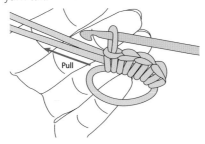

To start your next round, work your next stitch in the first single crochet of the completed adjustable ring. For patterns that require a semi-circle base shape (like for an ear), you will be asked to turn the work so that the back of the piece faces you before you make a turning chain and begin working the next row in your pattern.

Working Around a Chain

When working around a chain of stitches, you'll first work in the back ridge loops of the chain and then in the front side of the chain to create your first round.
1 Make a chain per the pattern instructions. To begin round 1, work your first stitch in the back ridge loop of the 2nd chain from your hook. Mark this stitch with a place marker to make it easier to find when you are ready to begin round 2. Work the rest of the stitches indicated into the back ridge loops of the chain until you've reached the last chain above the slipknot. Work the indicated number of stitches into the back ridge loop of this last chain.

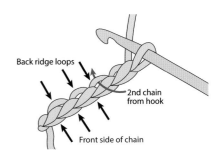

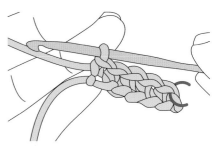

2 When you're ready to work the other side of the chain, rotate your work so the front side of the chain faces up. Starting in the next chain, insert your hook under the front side of the chain to work your next stitch.

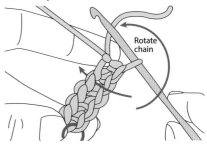

3 Continue working in the front sides of the remaining chains. Once the round is complete, continue on to round 2 (indicated by your stitch marker).

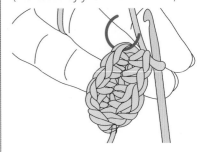

Working in a Chain Space (ch sp)

Proceed with making your next stitch as you normally would, but in this instance, work your stitches into the space below the chain.

Right Side (RS)/Wrong Side (WS)

When working in the round, the side of your pattern perceived as the "right side" will affect which part of the stitch is the back loop versus the front loop. The 6" tail left over from forming the adjustable ring will usually be on the wrong side of the piece. The same can be said for patterns that begin by working around a chain, provided you hold the 6" yarn tail at the back of your work as you crochet the first round.

Changing Colors

Work the stitch before the color change up until when you would normally draw the yarn through the loop(s) on your hook to complete the stitch.

To change colors, yarn over the hook with your new color and draw the new color through the remaining loop(s) on your hook, completing the stitch. You can then continue on to the next stitch in the new color.

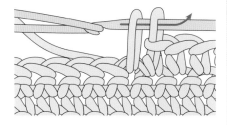

For color changes at the beginning of a new row, complete the stitch in your previous row and turn your work. Introduce the new color when you make your turning chain. Continue to work with your new color for the next row.

For color changes that take place in a slip stitch, simply insert the hook into the old color stitch, yarn over with the new color, and draw the new color through the loop on your hook to complete your slip stitch and the color change.

Working in Surface Stitches

Some patterns have details like skirts, sleeves, and boot cuffs that are created by crocheting onto the surface stitches of your pieces. This technique will usually be worked in raised loops that will be visible after you've worked a round in the back loops of your stitches or in the front posts.

For these details, take care to orient your work as indicated so the additional rounds of surface stitches will lie properly against your work.
1 Begin by locating which round you will be working in. Insert your hook under the exposed loop(s) on the surface of your work. Rejoin your yarn with a yarn over and pull the yarn through the surface stitch.

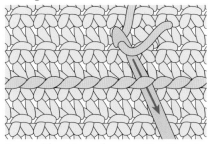

Exposed front loops from working bl sc sts

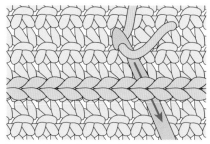

Exposed loops from working FPsc sts

2 Chain 1 and apply a stitch (like a single crochet) into the same surface loop you started in. This will create your first surface stitch.

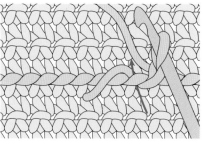

You can then continue to work in the remaining surface stitches in the round.

FINISHING STITCHES

Once your pattern pieces are complete, you can assemble and embellish your ornaments with just a handful of basic stitches. To ensure all the final details end up in the right spots, look over the photos for each ornament before you begin assembling them and use marking pins to help you work out the placement of your pattern pieces before sewing them together.

Leave long yarn tails when you fasten off the last rounds of your arm and leg pieces. When assembling, use marking pins to attach all your limbs to the body to ensure everything is even and balanced. Then, using the leftover yarn tails, place a single stitch at each marking pin to hold your pieces in place. Remove the pins and finish sewing your pieces down using a whip or mattress stitch.

Whip Stitch

Use this stitch to close flat seams. Hold the edges of your work together and, using your tapestry needle and yarn, draw the yarn through the edges before looping the yarn over the top of your work and back through the edges again in a spiral-like motion. Continue until the seam is closed or the piece is attached.

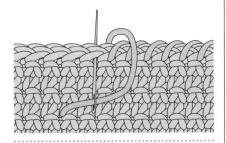

Mattress Stitch

The mattress stitch provides a nice tight seam when sewing crochet surfaces together, like a head to the open edges of a neck.

Choose a point on the surface or edge of your first piece and insert the needle from A to B under a single stitch and pull the yarn through. Cross over to the opposite surface and draw your needle under a single stitch from C to D with the entry point at C lining up between points A and B on the first

surface. Return to the first surface and insert your needle directly next to exit point B. Continue to work back and forth in this manner until seam is closed, pulling firmly after every few stitches to ensure a clean, closed seam.

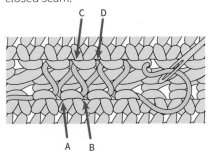

Closing Round Holes

For closing round holes like the ones at the last rounds of heads and body shapes, start by threading the remaining yarn tail onto a tapestry needle. Following the edge of the round opening, insert the needle through just the front loops of each stitch, effectively winding the yarn tail around the front loops of the stitches. When you've worked all the way around the opening, pull the tail firmly to close the hole (just like you were cinching a drawstring bag closed).

Long Stitch

Use this stitch to help shape the surface of your ornament. With your yarn and tapestry needle, draw the yarn up through the surface of your piece (1) and then reinsert the needle in a different location (2). Repeat if desired to double or triple up the yarn. To cinch the surface of your piece for details like toes or lip clefts, pull the yarn firmly as you work.

Up at 1, down at 2.

Running Stitch

Use this stitch to attach felt pieces or flattened crochet pieces to your work. To apply this stitch, draw your yarn or thread in and out of the surface(s) of your piece in a dashed line pattern.

Satin Stitch

Apply satin stitches by grouping short- or medium-length stitches closely together to build up a shape or fill an area with color.

Chain Stitch

1 Start by making a small stitch on the surface of your work. Bring the needle up through your work about a stitch length away, pass the needle through the small stitch, and reinsert the needle into its starting point. This is your first chain.

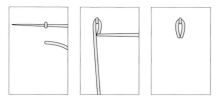

2 Bring your needle up through your work a stitch below your last chain. Slide the needle under your last chain and reinsert the needle into its starting point. Repeat.

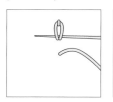

Lazy Daisy/Overcast Stitch

This stitch can be adjusted to create tight petal shapes or wider curved shapes like eyebrows or mouths. Begin by drawing the yarn up through the surface of your piece at (A) and then reinsert the needle at (B), leaving the yarn loose to achieve the desired level of curve. Choose a point along the curved long stitch and draw up the yarn at (C) and reinsert at (D) to hold the shape of the long stitch in place. Feel free to repeat if desired at other points along the long stitch if needed.

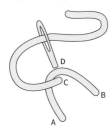

Couching

This technique involves sewing down piece of thicker yarn running along the top of the surface of your work with a thinner thread. Place and pose your yarn on the surface of your work, then use a needle and thread to intermittently sew a stitch over the yarn to hold its shaping in place. This stitch can be used to create effects like piped icing on cookies.

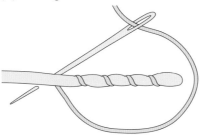

Try this trick to reduce the hassle of dealing with yarn ends when adding embroidery details!

Begin by inserting your needle about an inch from where you intend to start your embroidery and leave a 4" tail. Bring the needle up at the first stitch. Hold the yarn tail down with your fingers as you work the first couple of stitches until the yarn appears to feel secure. When you finish your last stitch, bring the needle out at the same spot of the beginning tail and cut the end, leaving another 4" tail. Knot the 2 yarn tails together, and then use a crochet hook or tapestry needle to draw the yarn and the knot back through the hole with a firm tug. Trim any visible yarn tails if needed.

Fringe Knots

Add a little hair to your character! Insert your hook through a surface stitch on your work and fold a 4" piece of yarn over the hook. Draw the yarn halfway through the surface stitch to create a small loop. Proceed to pull the loose ends of the yarn through this loop and pull tightly to secure it. For a fuzzier look, use a steel tapestry needle to separate the yarn plys and fluff them with your fingers or a fine toothed comb. Trim as needed.

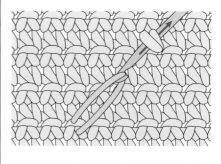
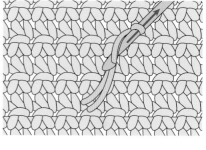
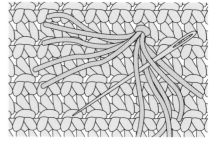

ORNAMENT HANGERS

Beautiful ornaments deserve special hangers. With just a few simple wire-working tools, some beads, and a couple of spools of jewelry wire, your ornaments can be hanging pretty on a lovely set of custom hooks.

RIBBON AND TWINE ALSO MAKE LOVELY HANGING LOOPS FOR ORNAMENTS AS WELL! YOU CAN EVEN SLIP A FEW BEADS ONTO A LOOP OF RIBBON AND SECURE THEM WITH A KNOT.

After you attach the jump ring to your ornament, thread ribbon or twine through the ring and tie the ends in a bow. To keep the bow ends from fraying, cut the ends of the ribbons ⅛" to ¼" longer than needed and apply a light coating of craft glue to just the underside of the ribbon ends with your finger. Allow glue to dry, then trim the glue-coated ribbon ends to their final length.

GETTING STARTED

To create your own wire hangers, you will need the following tools and materials.

- Wire cutters (Hakko recommended)
- Fine round-nose pliers (Beadsmith recommended)
- Flat/duck bill pliers (Beadsmith recommended)
- Jewelry wire (16 gauge)
- Jewelry wire (20 gauge)
- Assorted beads
- 8 mm–10 mm jump rings

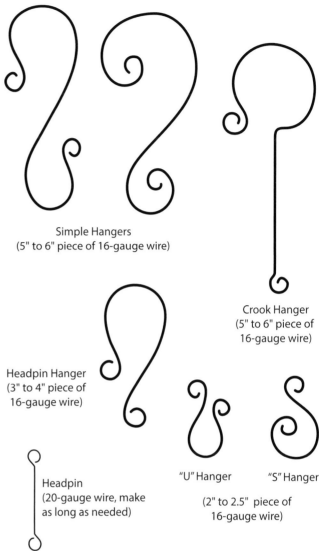

Simple Hangers
(5" to 6" piece of 16-gauge wire)

Crook Hanger
(5" to 6" piece of
16-gauge wire)

Headpin Hanger
(3" to 4" piece of
16-gauge wire)

Headpin
(20-gauge wire, make
as long as needed)

"U" Hanger

"S" Hanger

(2" to 2.5" piece of
16-gauge wire)

PRACTICE MAKES PERFECT

If you are new to working with wire (like I was when I started this chapter), it's likely your first 2, 3, or 10 hangers may not be perfect. It takes practice, like anything else!

ATTACH A JUMP RING

Give your ornament a sturdy hanging point by sewing a jump ring onto the surface of your work. To check your hanging point before you attach the jump ring, hook the point where you want to attach your jump ring with your needle or crochet hook and allow your work to be suspended on the needle or hook to see how it balances (and whether you need to adjust that location).

WIRE BENDING TIPS

For the larger "Simple," "Crook," and "Headpin" hangers, cut a piece of 16-gauge wire to the length suggested on the template you wish to follow. Begin by creating one of the loops at the end of the wire by holding the end in your round-nose pliers and bending the wire around the pliers (versus twisting the pliers to bend the wire). Once you have your loop, hold the wire with your flat/duck bill pliers and gently bend the wire with your fingers.

Chances are, you will end up with some sharp and bumpy crimp points in the wires' curves as you work. Leave them for now and focus on getting the general shape. Once the main curves are in, trim off any excess and use round-nose pliers to bend the loop at the other end of the wire.

To smooth out your crimps and reshape your curves, draw your flat/duck bill pliers over the problem areas, clamping the pliers up and down as you move to reshape and smooth out the wire. Lay the hanger on top of the

template to check the shape as you work. Keep on clamping and moving over the wire until you are happy with the shape.

For the beaded section of the headpin hanger, cut a length of 20-gauge wire and straighten it out. Bend a loop on one end. Thread beads onto the headpin. Cut the remaining wire to roughly ⅜" from the last bead and twist the end into a loop with your round-nose pliers to secure the beads.

For the "Crook" hanger, thread the beads onto the straight section of the hanger. Cut the remaining wire to roughly ⅜" from the last bead and twist the end into a loop to secure the beads. With your flat pliers, twist the loop at the bottom of the crook so it is perpendicular to the rest of the hanger.

For the smaller "U" and "S" hangers, apply the small loops to both ends of the wire before bending the wire into its final shape. They can then be added as the bottom link on the "Headpin" and "Crook" hangers.

CUSTOMIZING AND PERSONALIZING

Try customizing the beads on your hanger with a date or monogram to celebrate a special event.

To customize wooden beads, you will need:

• 20 mm wooden coin beads (available on Etsy and online bead stores)
• Oil-based metallic extra-fine paint pens
• Number and/or letter stickers

Stickers: Consider bringing your beads with you when picking out stickers (so you know they will fit). Stickers can also be applied to a variety of other bead shapes and materials, so let your imagination run wild!

Metallic Paint Pens: When using paint pens, the metallic extra-fine type seems to bleed less than the white one. Trace your bead onto a sheet of paper and practice what you want to paint before you begin.

When painting on the surface of a wooden coin bead, keep an eye out for rough surfaces that might cause the paint to bleed when applied. Mistakes can be mostly wiped away if done quickly while the paint is still wet. To hide a mistake, consider covering the wiped side with a sticker and redo lettering on the other side of the bead.

Here's a few more ideas to customize your ornament hangers:

• Custom punched copper tags from Etsy
• Bakeable clay, such as Sculpey. **Option 1:** Roll out beads, flatten the surface, and run them through with a toothpick before you stamp with solvent-type ink and bake. **Option 2:** Flatten out a sheet of clay, stamp with solvent-type ink, cut out the bead, bake, and then drill a hole.
• Chipboard or chalk board gift tags with glittery stickers

NORTH POLE

THE NORTH POLE IS

bustling

WITH ELVES MAKING TOYS.

Christmas

IS JUST AROUND

THE CORNER!

SANTA

······ INTERMEDIATE • FINISHED SIZE: 3" TALL, 2¼" WIDE ······

⸓ MATERIALS ⸓

- Sock weight yarn in black, green, ivory, red, tan, and white
- Hook size C (2.75 mm)
- Tapestry needle
- Scissors
- Polyester fiberfill
- Black felt
- Gold/yellow felt
- Craft glue or needle and thread
- (1) 10 mm jump ring

HEAD AND BODY

Starting with tan, make a 6-st adjustable ring.

Rnd 1: Sc 2 in each st around. (12 sts)

Rnd 2: *Sc 2, sc 2 in next st; rep from * 3 more times. (16 sts)

Rnds 3-4: Sc 16.

Rnd 5: *Sc 2, sc2tog; rep from * 3 more times. (12 sts)

Change to red.

Rnd 6: In bl, *sc 2, sc 2 in next st; rep from * 3 more times. (16 sts)

Rnd 7: *Sc 3, sc 2 in next st; rep from * 3 more times. (20 sts)

Rnd 8: *Sc 3, sc 2 in next st; rep from * 4 more times. (25 sts)

Rnd 9: *Sc 4, sc 2 in next st; rep from * 4 more times. (30 sts)

Rnd 10: Sc 30.

Rnd 11: *Sc 3, sc2tog; rep from * 5 more times. (24 sts)

Rnd 12: BPsc 24.

Rnd 13: *Sc 2, sc2tog; rep from * 5 more times. (18 sts)

Rnd 14: Sc2tog 9 times. (9 sts)

Stuff body.

Fasten off yarn, close hole, and weave in yarn.

NECK TRIM DETAIL

Rnd 1: With head pointed down and using white yarn, (sl st 1, ch 1, hdc 1) in one of the exposed fls of rnd 5 (counts as first hdc). Cont to work in the exposed fls of rnd 5; hdc 4, hdc 2 in next st, ch 6. Starting in 2nd ch from hook and working in back ridge loops, hdc in next 5 chs. Cont to work in the exposed fls of rnd 5; hdc 2 in next st, hdc 5.

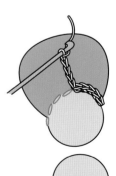

Fasten off yarn in first hdc st and cut yarn, leaving long tail for sewing.

Flatten the collar and front coat trim against the body and sew in place with leftover yarn tail.

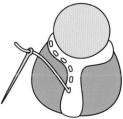

SANTA *(continued)*

COAT TRIM DETAIL

Rnd 1: With head pointed up and using white yarn, (sl st 1, ch 1, hdc 1) in one of the exposed loops of rnd 12 (counts as first hdc). Cont to work 1 hdc in each of the 23 remaining exposed loops of rnd 12. (24 sts)

Cut a ¼" by 4½" strip from black felt. Wrap around body above coat trim detail for a belt, trim to fit, and secure the ends in the back.

With gold/yellow felt, cut out (1) ¼" by ⅜" rectangle. Attach rectangle to the front of the belt.

HAND AND ARM (MAKE 2)

Starting with green, make a 3-st adjustable ring.

Rnd 1: *Sc 2 in each st around. (6 sts)

Rnd 2: Sc 6.

Change to red.

Rnd 3: FPsc 6.

Rnd 4: In bl, sc 6.

Rnds 5-6: Sc 6.

Fasten off yarn. Weave yarn tail through fls of rnd 6 and pull to close.

SLEEVE TRIM DETAIL

Rnd 1: With hand pointed up and using white yarn, (sl st 1, ch 1, sc 1) in one of the exposed fls of rnd 3 (counts as first sc). Cont to work 1 sc in each of the 5 remaining exposed fls of rnd 3. (6 sts)

Fasten off yarn and weave in end.

Sew arms to shoulders of the body. With red, tack the inside surfaces of the arms to the body to keep them from splaying out.

LEG (MAKE 2)

Starting with black, make a 6-st adjustable ring.

Rnd 1: (Boot opening) In bl, sc 2, ch 3, sk 3, sc 1. (6 sts)

Rnd 2: Sc 2, sc in each st of ch-3, sc 1. (6 sts)

Rnd 3: Sc 6.

Change to red.

Rnd 4: In bl, sc 6.

Rnd 5: Sc 6.

Fasten off yarn, leaving a long tail for sewing.

BOOT

In black.

Rnd 1: Starting in lower right corner of boot opening, reattach yarn (sl st, ch 1, sc 1) in same st (counts as first sc) and cont to sc in the remaining 5 sts around the inside of the boot opening. (6 sts)

Rnd 2: Sc 6.

Fasten off yarn, leaving a long tail. Lightly stuff boot and leg and close hole. Use leftover yarn tail to patch any holes in the sides of the boot.

BOOT CUFF DETAIL

Rnd 1: With boot pointed down and using black yarn, (sl st 1, ch 1, sc 1) in one of the exposed fls of rnd 3 (counts as first sc). Cont to work 1 sc in each of the 5 remaining exposed fls of rnd 3. (6 sts)

Fasten off yarn and weave in end. Fold boot cuff down.

Sew open edges of legs to bottom of body.

HAT

Starting with red, make a 3-st adjustable ring.

Rnd 1: Sc 1, sc 2 in next st, sc 1. (4 sts)

Rnd 2: Sc 2, sc 2 in next st, sc 1. (5 sts)

Rnd 3: Sc 2, sc 2 in next st, sc 2. (6 sts)

Rnd 4: *Sc 2, sc 2 in next st; rep from * 1 more time. (8 sts)

Rnd 5: *Sc 3, sc 2 in next st; rep from * 1 more time. (10 sts)

Rnd 6: *Sc 4, sc 2 in next st; rep from * 1 more time. (12 sts)

Rnds 7-8: Sl st 2, sc 1, hdc 6, sc 1, sl st 2.

Rnd 9: *Sc 2, sc 2 in next st; rep from * 3 more times. (16 sts)

Rnd 10: *Sc 3, sc 2 in next st; rep from * 3 more times. (20 sts)

Change to white.

Rnd 11: FPhdc 20.

Rnd 12: BPsc 20.

Fasten off yarn.

With the hdc sts from rnd 7-8 facing front, place hat onto head so only 2 rnds of the face area are visible. The white trim of the hat should touch the white trim of the coat at the back of the neck. Sew hat down to head. Tack the tip of the hat down on the side of the head.

Cut (13 to 15) 6" pieces of ivory and use a fringe knot to attach them to the bottom edge of the face for a beard. Separate yarn plys with tapestry needle, fluff with fingers, and trim to desired length.

NOSE

In tan, make a 4-st adjustable ring.

Rnd 1: Sc 2 in each st around. (8 sts)

Rnd 2: *Sc 2, sc2tog; rep from * 1 more time. (6 sts)

Fasten off yarn and attach open edge of nose to upper half of face.

MUSTACHE

In ivory. Leave a long yarn tail at the beginning of work.

Row 1: *Ch 3, sl st in back ridge loop of 3rd ch from hook; rep from * 1 more time. Turn. (2 ch-3 sps)

Row 2: Ch 1, (sl st 1, sc 1, ch 2, sl st in back ridge loop of 2nd ch from hook, hdc 1, sl st 1) in first ch-3 sp, (sl st 1, hdc 1, ch 2, sl st in back ridge loop of 2nd ch from hook, sc 1, sl st 1) in 2nd ch-3 sp.

Fasten off yarn, leaving a 2nd long yarn tail.

Attach mustache directly under nose using 1 of the yarn tails. Once mustache is secured, draw both leftover yarn tails up and out through the tip of the hat. Tie a knot at the base of yarn tails and trim to about ¼" long. Separate the yarn plys with a tapestry needle and fluff with your fingers.

Attach hanging loop (page 18).

MRS. CLAUS

······ INTERMEDIATE • FINISHED SIZE: 3" TALL, 2" WIDE ······

⇒ MATERIALS ⇒

- Sock weight yarn in black, dark brown, ivory, red, tan, and white
- Hook size C (2.75 mm)
- Tapestry needle
- Scissors
- Polyester fiberfill
- Craft glue or needle and thread
- Place marker
- (1) 10 mm jump ring

HEAD AND BODY

Starting with tan, make an 6-st adjustable ring.

Rnd 1: Sc 2 in each st around. (12 sts)

Rnd 2: *Sc 2, sc 2 in next st; rep from * 3 more times. (16 sts)

Rnds 3-5: Sc 16.

Rnd 6: *Sc 2, sc2tog; rep from * 3 more times. (12 sts)

Stuff head.

Rnd 7: Sc2tog 6 times. (6 sts)

Change to red.

Rnd 8: In bl, *sc 2, sc 2 in next st; rep from * 1 more time. (8 sts)

Rnd 9: Sc 2 in each st around. (16 sts)

Rnd 10: *Sc 1, sc 2 in next st; rep from * 7 more times. (24 sts)

Rnd 11: Sc2tog 3 times, sc 6, pm, sc 6, sc2tog 3 times. (18 sts)

Rnd 12: *Sc 1, sc2tog; rep from * 5 more times. (12 sts)

Rnd 13: Sc 2 in each st around. (24 sts)

Rnd 14: *Sc 3, sc 2 in next st; rep from * 5 more times. (30 sts)

Rnd 15: *Sc 4, sc 2 in next st; rep from * 5 more times. (36 sts)

Rnd 16: Sc 36.

Rnd 17: *Sc 4, sc2tog; rep from * 5 more times. (30 sts)

Rnd 18: Sc 30.

Rnd 19: BPsc 30.

Rnd 20: *Sc 1, sc2tog; rep from * 9 more times. (20 sts)

Rnd 21: Sc2tog 10 times. (10 sts)

Stuff body. Fasten off yarn and close hole. The marker indicates the front of the body.

COLLAR DETAIL

Rnd 1: With head pointed up and using red yarn, (sl st 1, ch 1, sc 1) in one of the exposed fls rnd 7 (counts as first sc). Cont to work 1 sc in each of the 5 remaining exposed fls of rnd 7. (6 sts)

Fasten off yarn and weave in ends.

MRS. CLAUS *(continued)*

DRESS TRIM DETAIL

Rnd 1: With head pointed up and using white yarn, (sl st 1, ch 1, hdc 2) in one of the exposed loops of rnd 19 (counts as first hdc inc). Cont to work 2 hdc in each of the 29 remaining exposed loops of rnd 19. (60 sts)

Fasten off yarn and weave in ends.

SHOE (MAKE 2)

With dark brown, make a 4-st adjustable ring.

Rnd 1: *Sc 1, sc 2 in next st; rep from * 1 more time. (6 sts)

Rnds 2-3: Sc 6.

Stuff foot lightly and close hole in the back of the foot. Sew feet to underside of dress.

APRON

With white, make a 6-st adjustable ring and turn. Do not join ring.

Row 1: Ch 1, sc 1, sc 2 in next 4 sts, sc 1, turn. (10 sts)

Row 2: Ch 1, sc 1 (sc 1, ch 2, sc 1) in next 8 sts, sc 1. Do not turn. Work top panel of apron next.

TOP PANEL OF APRON

Sc 5 sts across the top edge of the apron, pm, turn.

Rows 3-4: Ch 1, sc 5, turn. (5 sts)

APRON NECK STRAP

Ch 10 and fasten off yarn.

APRON WAIST STRAPS

With white, (sl st, ch 1) in edge of apron next to pm, ch 13 more and fasten off yarn.

Make a 2nd ch 14 strap on the opposite side of apron and fasten off. Trim the excess yarn to about ¼" for a small tassel at the end of each apron waist strap.

Place apron against the body and draw the neck strap around the back of the head and shoulders to the opposite corner of the apron top panel. Sew strap in place. Wrap the apron waist straps behind the body and tie them together in a square knot. If desired, use white to tack down the front edge of the apron to the body to keep it laying flat.

HAIR

In ivory, make a 4-st adjustable ring.

Rnd 1: Sc 2 in each st around. (8 sts)

Rnd 2: Sc2tog 4 times. (4 sts)

Rnd 3: Sc 2 in each st around. (8 sts)

Rnd 4: Sc 2 in each st around. (16 sts)

Rnd 5: *Sc 3, sc 2 in next st; rep from * 3 more times. (20 sts)

Rnd 6: Sc 4, sl st 1, sk 1, sl st 1, sk 1, (sl st 1, hdc 2) in next st, (hdc 1, sc 1) in next st, sl st 1, (sc 1, hdc 1) in next st, (hdc 2, st st 1) in next st, sk 1, sl st 1, sk 1, sl st 1, sc 3. (22 sts)

Rnd 7: Sl st 1, sc 2 in next st, sl st 1, sk 1, sl st 1, sk 1, sl st 1, sc 4, sl st 1, sc 4, sl st 1, sk 1, sl st 1, sk 1, sl st 1, sc 2 in next st. (20 sts)

Place the hair on the head and sew the edge down with small running sts.

Attach hanging loop (page 18).

HAND AND ARM (MAKE 2)

Starting with tan, make a 3-st adjustable ring.

Rnd 1: * Sc 2 in each st around. (6 sts)

Rnd 2: *Sc 1, sc2tog; rep from * 1 more time. (4 sts)

Stuff hand. Change to red.

Rnd 3: FPsc 4.

Rnd 4: Sc 2 in each st around. (8 sts)

Rnd 5: Sc 8.

Rnd 6: *Sc 2, sc2tog; rep from * 1 more time. (6 sts)

Rnd 7: Sc 6.

Fasten off yarn and stuff arm lightly. Close hole at top of arm.

Sew the arms to the shoulders of the body. Tack the hands down to the front of the apron.

REINDEER

······ INTERMEDIATE • FINISHED SIZE: 3½" TALL, 2" LONG, 1½" WIDE ······

≑ MATERIALS ≑

- Sock weight yarn in black, dark brown, ivory, and tan
- Hook size C (2.75 mm)
- Tapestry needle
- Scissors
- Polyester fiberfill
- (2) 4 mm plastic eyes
- Red felt
- (8) Gold 6/0 "E" beads
- Craft glue or needle and thread
- (1) 10 mm jump ring

HEAD

In tan, make an 8-st adjustable ring.

Rnd 1: Sc 2 in each st around. (16 sts)

Rnd 2: *Sc 3, sc 2 in next st; rep from * 3 more times. (20 sts)

Rnds 3-5: Sc 20.

Rnd 6: *Sc 3, sc2tog; rep from * 3 more times. (16 sts)

Rnd 7: *Sc 2, sc2tog; rep from * 3 more times. (12 sts)

Stuff head.

Rnd 8: Sc2tog 6 times.

Fasten off yarn and close hole at the top of the head.

BODY

In tan, make a 5-st adjustable ring.

Rnd 1: Sc 2 in each st around. (10 sts)

Rnd 2: *Sc 1, sc 2 in next st; rep from * 4 more times. (15 sts)

Rnd 3: (Neck opening) Sc 5, ch 5, sk 5, sc 5. (15 sts)

Rnd 4: Sc 5, sc in each st of ch-5, sc 5. (15 sts)

Rnds 5-7: Sc 15.

Rnd 8: *Sc 3, sc2tog; rep from * 2 more times. (12 sts)

Rnd 9: Sc2tog 6 times. (6 sts)

Fasten off yarn and close hole.

NECK

Rnd 1: In tan, (sl st 1, ch 1, sc 1) in one of the sts of the neck opening (counts as first sc). Cont to work 1 sc in each of the remaining 9 sts around the inside of the neck opening. (10 sts)

Rnds 2-4: Sc 10.

Fasten off yarn, leaving a long tail. Stuff body.

Attach bottom of the head to the open neck edge. Use leftover yarn tails to close any holes that may appear in the corners in rnd 1 of the neck.

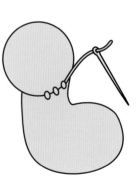

REINDEER *(continued)*

MUZZLE

In ivory, make a 6-st adjustable ring.

Rnd 1: *Hdc 2, hdc 2 in next st; rep from * 1 more time. (8 sts) Fasten off yarn.

Sew open edge of muzzle to front of head. Glue or sew 4 mm plastic eyes or beads to the face just above the muzzle. In black, apply a nose in satin sts. Using a single yarn ply from your black yarn or black embroidery thread, apply 1 short st above each eye for an eyebrow.

EAR AND TAIL (MAKE 3)

In tan, make a 5-st adjustable ring.

Rnd 1: Sc 2, (sc 1, hdc 1, ch 3, sl st in back ridge loop of 3rd ch from hook, hdc 1, sc 1) in next st, sc 2. Fasten off yarn.

Attach round end of ears to sides of head and the pointy end to the back of body.

ANTLER (MAKE 2)

In dark brown, ch-9.

Starting in 2nd ch from hook and working in back ridge loops, sl st 4, *ch 3. Starting in 2nd ch from hook and working in back ridge loops, sl st 2, cont working in ch-9, sl st 2; rep from * 1 more time. Fasten off yarn, leaving a long tail for sewing.

Attach antlers to top of head.

LEG (MAKE 4)

In dark brown, make a 5-st adjustable ring.

Rnd 1: Sc 2 in each st around. (10 sts)

Rnd 2: In bl, sc 10.

Rnd 3: *Sc 3, sc2tog; rep from * 1 more time. (8 sts)

Stuff hoof.

Change to ivory.

Rnd 4: FPsc 8.

Change to tan.

Rnd 5: *Sc 2, sc2tog; rep from * 1 more time. (6 sts)

Rnds 6-8: Sc 6.

Close hole at top of leg. Attach legs to shoulders and hips of body. Tack the insides of the legs to the body to keep legs from splaying out.

Cut 12 pieces of ivory and attach to the chest below the neck using fringe knots. Cut short and separate yarn plys with a tapestry needle and/or fingers to make the yarn fuzzy.

HARNESS

Cut (2) red felt strips ¼" wide by 5" long. Wrap one strip around the front chest and glue or sew it to the sides of the body. Wrap the other strip around the middle of the body (covering up the attachment points of the first strip) and glue or sew in place. Sew gold 6/0 seed beads to the harness for bells.

Attach hanging loop (page 18) to the back of the head.

ELF

······ INTERMEDIATE • FINISHED SIZE: 2½" TALL, 1¾" WIDE ······

MATERIALS

- Sock weight yarn in dark brown, green, red, and tan
- Hook size C (2.75 mm)
- (1) 6 mm gold bead
- Tapestry needle
- Scissors
- Polyester fiberfill
- Black felt
- Gold/yellow felt
- Craft glue or needle and thread
- (1) 10 mm jump ring

HEAD AND BODY

Starting with tan, make a 6-st adjustable ring.

Rnd 1: Sc 2 in each st around. (12 sts)

Rnd 2-3: Sc 12.

Change to green.

Rnd 4: In bl, *sc 2, sc 2 in next st; rep from * 3 more times. (16 sts)

Rnd 5: Sc 16.

Rnd 6: *Sc 7, sc 2 in next st; rep from * 1 more time. (18 sts)

Rnd 7 : Sc 18.

Rnd 8: BPsc 18.

Rnd 9: *Sc 1, sc2tog; rep from * 5 more times. (12 sts)

Fasten off yarn, stuff body, and close hole.

COLLAR DETAIL

Rnd 1: With head pointed up and using green yarn, (sl st 1, ch 1, FPsc) in one of the stitch posts directly below the exposed fls of rnd 3 (counts as first FPsc). Cont to work 1 FPsc in each of the 15 remaining stitch posts directly below the exposed fls of rnd 3. (16 sts)

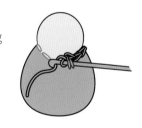

Fasten off yarn and weave in ends.

JACKET TRIM DETAIL

Rnd 1: With head pointed down and using green yarn, (sl st 1, ch 1, sc 1) in one of the exposed loops of rnd 8 (counts as first sc). Cont to work 1 sc in each of the 17 remaining exposed loops of rnd 8. (18 sts)

Cut out (1) ¼" by 4" strip from black felt. Wrap around body above jacket trim detail for a belt, trim to fit, and secure the ends in the back.

With gold/yellow felt, cut out (1) ¼" by ⅜" rectangle. Attach rectangle to the front of the belt.

ELF *(continued)*

NOSE

In tan, make a 4-st adjustable ring.

Rnd 1: *Sc 1, sc 2 in each st; rep from * 1 more time. (6 sts)

Rnd 2: *Sc 1, sc2tog; rep from * 1 more time. (4 sts)

Fasten off yarn and attach open edge of nose to face.

HAT

In red, make a 3-st adjustable ring.

Rnd 1: Sc 1, sc 2 in next st, sc 1. (4 sts)

Rnd 2: Sc 2, sc 2 in next st, sc 1. (5 sts)

Rnd 3: Sc 2, Sc 2 in next st, sc 2. (6 sts)

Rnd 4: *Sc 2, sc 2 in next st; rep from * 1 more time. (8 sts)

Rnd 5: *Sc 3, sc 2 in next st; rep from * 1 more time. (10 sts)

Rnd 6: *Sc 4, sc 2 in next st; rep from * 1 more time. (12 sts)

Rnd 7: *Sc 5, sc 2 in next st; rep from * 1 more time. (14 sts)

Rnd 8: Sc 14.

Fasten off yarn, leaving a long tail for sewing.

Stuff hat lightly. Cover the entire elf head and face except for the nose and sew in place.

With red, apply a line of running sts along the side of the hat from the top to the base. Pull the yarn tails firmly to curve the top half of the hat to one side. Apply a 6 mm gold bead to the tip of the hat for a bell.

HAND AND ARM (MAKE 2)

Starting with tan, make a 3-st adjustable ring.

Rnd 1: *Sc 2 in each st around. (6 sts)

Rnd 2: Sc 6.

Change to green.

Rnd 3: FPsc 6.

Rnd 4: In bl, sc 6.

Rnd 5: Sc 6.

Fasten off yarn. Close hole.

Sew arms to shoulders of the body. With green, tack the inside surfaces of the arms to the body to keep them from splaying out.

EAR (MAKE 2)

In tan, make a 4-st adjustable ring. Turn. Do not join ring.

Row 1: Ch 1, sl st 3, (hdc, dc, hdc) in next st.

Fasten off yarn, leaving a long tail for sewing.

Attach ears to sides of head over the hat.

SHOE (MAKE 2)

In dark brown, make a 4-st adjustable ring.

Rnd 1: *Sc 1, sc 2 in next st; rep from * 1 more time. (6 sts)

Rnd 2-3: Sc 6.

Rnd 4: Sc2tog 3 times. (3 sts)

Rnd 5: Ch 5, sc2tog, and fasten off yarn.

With the ch-5 loops at the fronts of the shoes pointed forward, attach the tops of the shoes to the bottom of the body.

Attach hanging loop (page 18).

STOCKING

······ EASY • FINISHED SIZE: 2¾" TALL, 2" WIDE ······

÷ MATERIALS ÷

- Sock weight yarn in ivory and red
- Hook size C (2.75 mm)
- Tapestry needle
- Scissors
- (1) 10 mm jump ring

Starting with ivory, make a 6-st adjustable ring.

Rnd 1: Sc 2 in each st around. (12 sts)

Rnd 2: *Sc 1, sc 2 in next st; rep from * 5 more times. (18 sts)

Rnds 3-4: Sc 18.

Change to red.

Rnd 5: *Sc 7, sc2tog; rep from * 1 more time. (16 sts)

Rnd 6-7: Sc 16.

Row 8: Sc 16, turn.

Row 9: Ch 1, sc 8, turn.

Change to ivory.

Rows 10-12: Ch 1, sc 8, turn.

Row 13: Ch 1, *sc 1, sc2tog, sc 1; rep from * 1 more time, turn.

Row 14: Ch 1, sc2tog, sc 2, sc2tog, turn.

Row 15: Ch 1, sc2tog 2 times, turn.

Change to red.

Rnd 16: Sk ch 1, sc 2, pick up 4 sc sts along the ivory edge, sc 8, pick up 4 sc sts along the ivory edge. (18 sts)

Rnds 17-22: Sc 18.

Change to ivory.

Rnds 23-28: Sc 18.

Rnd 29: *Sl st 1, ch 2; rep from * to end.

Fasten off yarn, leaving a long tail for sewing.

Fold over ivory part and sew in place with a few sts.

Attach hanging loop (page 18).

IF YOU WOULD LIKE TO ADD A MOUSE TO YOUR STOCKING, CHECK OUT MITTEN MOUSE ON PAGE 83.

PRESENT

······ EASY • FINISHED SIZE: 1½" TALL, 2" WIDE ······

⇌ MATERIALS ⇌

- Sock weight yarn in aqua
- Hook size C (2.75 mm)
- Blue felt (for lined box)
- Polyester fiberfill (for stuffed box)
- (60") ⅜" ribbon
- Craft glue or needle and thread
- Tapestry needle
- Scissors
- (1) 10 mm jump ring

BOX

In aqua, make a 4-st adjustable ring.

Rnd 1: Sc 3 in each st around. (12 sts)

Rnd 2: *Sc 1, sc 3 in next st, sc 1; rep from * 3 more times. (20 sts)

Rnd 3: *Sc 2, sc 3 in next st, sc 2; rep from * 3 more times. (28 sts)

Rnd 4: BPsc 28.

Rnds 5-11: Sc 28.

Fasten off yarn and weave in ends.

BOX LID

In aqua, make a 4-st adjustable ring.

Rnd 1: Sc 3 in each st around. (12 sts)

Rnd 2: *Sc 1, sc 3 in next st, sc 1; rep from * 3 more times. (20 sts)

Rnd 3: *Sc 2, sc 3 in next st, sc 2; rep from * 3 more times. (28 sts)

Rnd 4: *Sc 3, sc 3 in next st, sc 3; rep from * 3 more times. (36 sts)

Rnd 5: BPsc 36.

Rnds 6-7: Sc 36.

Fasten off yarn and weave in ends.

FOR A STUFFED GIFT BOX

Cut (4) 8" pieces of ribbon. Sew or glue 2 pieces of ribbon to bottom and sides of the box and the top and sides of the box lid. Fold the ends of the ribbons under the lip of the lid and into the interior of the box, trim excess, then glue or sew in place. Lightly fill box with stuffing. Place lid on top of box and sew in place. To add a bow, see page 42.

THIS WORKING GIFT BOX CAN HOLD SOMETHING EXTRA SPECIAL TO HIDE AMONG YOUR CHRISTMAS TREE'S BRANCHES (NO PEEKING!!).

PRESENT *(continued)*

FOR A BOX THAT OPENS

From blue felt, cut out (1) ½" square and (4) 1½" by ⁵⁄₁₆"
strips for the box lid. Cut out (1) 1¼" square and (4) 1" by
1¼" squares for the box interior. Coat the back of each piece
of felt with craft glue and set aside to dry. Once dry, give the
felt a second coat of glue (on the same side as the first coat)
and apply the pieces to the bottom and side wall interiors of
the box and lid.

To help place the felt square in
the bottom of the box, invert
the box and press the square
of felt onto the floor of the box,
then invert the box again so the
felt square will be in the correct
position. Glue the remaining felt
squares to the interior walls
of the box and allow glue to
dry completely.

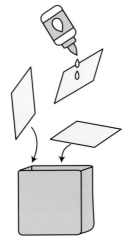

Cut (4) 8" pieces of ribbon. Sew
or glue 2 pieces of ribbon to
bottom and sides of the box and
the top and sides of the box lid.
Fold the ends of the ribbons under the lip of the lid and into
the interior of the box, trim excess, then glue or sew in place.

Tack down 2 corners of the box lid to the box to provide a
"hinge" point. The box should fit snugly enough into the lid
to hold the closed present together.

MAKE A BOW

To make a bow, cut (6 to 7) 2" pieces of ribbon and (8 to 9)
1½" pieces of ribbon. Apply a dab of glue to ribbon ends,
press ends tog, and allow loops to dry. With glued ends of
the loops pointed toward the center of the box lid, arrange
the larger loops in a circle on the top of the box lid. Glue or
sew down. Arrange a 2nd circle of smaller loops on top of
larger loops. Glue or sew down. Sew a hanging loop to the
center of the bow (page 18).

Stuffed box with bow   Hinged box with bow

CHRISTMAS TREE

······· EASY • FINISHED SIZE: 3½" TALL WITH STAR, 2" WIDE·······

⋛ MATERIALS ⋛

- Sock weight yarn in dark brown, green, ivory, and yellow
- (15–20) 6 mm gold metallic beads
- (20) Gold 11/0 seed beads
- Invisible thread
- Beading needle
- Hook size C (2.75 mm)
- Polyester fiberfill
- Tapestry needle
- Scissors
- (1) 10 mm jump ring

TREE

In dark brown, make a 4-st adjustable ring.

Rnds 1-3: Sc 4.

Change to green.

Rnd 4: In fl, sc 2 in each st around. (8 sts)

Rnd 5: Sc 2 in each st around. (16 sts)

Rnd 6: *Sc 1, sc 2 in next st; rep from * 7 more times. (24 sts)

Rnd 7: In bl, *sc 11, sc 2 in next st; rep from * 1 more time. (26 sts)

Rnd 8: In bl, hdc 26.

Rnd 9: In bl, *hdc 4, sk 1, hdc 1; rep from * 3 more times, hdc 2. (22 sts)

Rnd 10: In bl, *hdc 3, sk 1, hdc 1; rep from * 3 more times, hdc 2. (18 sts)

Rnd 11: In bl, *hdc 2, sk 1, hdc 1; rep from * 3 more times, hdc 2. (14 sts)

Rnd 12: In bl, hdc 14.

Rnd 13: In bl, hdc 1, *hdc 1, sk 1, hdc 1; rep from * 3 more times, hdc 1. (10 sts)

Rnd 14: In bl, sc 10.

Stuff tree.

Rnd 15: In bl, sc2tog 5 times. (5 sts)

Fasten off yarn and weave in ends.

CHRISTMAS TREE *(continued)*

BRANCHES DETAIL

With tree held upside down and using green yarn, (sl st 1, ch 1, sc 1) in the first exposed fl at the beginning of rnd 6. Cont working in the spiral of exposed fls on the surface of the tree in the following pattern; *Sl st 1, (sl st 1, sc 1, ch 2, sl st in base of ch 2) in next st, (sc 1, sl st 1) in next st; rep from * to the top of the tree.

Fasten off yarn and weave in ends.

GARLAND

In ivory make (1) ch each in 5", 6½", and 7½" lengths.

Load the chain onto your tapestry needle and weave the chain through the surface of your tree like a long running st. Once you have reached the beginning of the chain, distribute the chain evenly around the tree by loosing the swags of the garland with your fingers. Apply the 7½" ch in swags to the bottom 3rd of the tree. Apply the 6½" ch in swags to the middle 3rd of the tree. Apply the 5" ch in swags to the top 3rd of the tree.

more tree trimming options:

1. beaded garland option: string colorful or metallic seed beads together on invisible thread and apply to tree for a beaded garland.

2. tree light garland option: string colorful seed beads and green bugle beads (tube shaped beads) on invisible thread for a tree light garland.

3. puff paint and glitter: give your tree a coating of snow.

you can also apply a star-shaped bead to the top of your tree to finish your ornament.

STAR

In yellow, make a 5-st adjustable ring.

Rnd 1: *Sl st 1, ch 3, turn work 360° to twist ch-3, sl st in st at base of ch-3; rep from * 4 more times.

Fasten off yarn and sew star to top of tree.

If desired, sew gold seed beads around edge of the star with invisible thread and a beading needle.

Attach hanging loop (page 18).

CHRISTMAS GOODIES

THE KITCHEN IS

FILLED WITH

scrumptious

HOLIDAY BAKING SMELLS—

BETTER GET A

cookie

BEFORE

Santa

SNEAKS THEM ALL!

FIGGY PUDDING

······ BEGINNER • FINISHED SIZE: 2" WIDE, 2" TALL ······

⚜ MATERIALS ⚜

- Sock weight yarn in dark brown, green, ivory, and tan
- Hook size C (2.75 mm)
- (3) 6–7 mm red beads
- Marking pins
- Tapestry needle
- Scissors
- (1) 10 mm jump ring

PUDDING

With dark brown, make an 8-st adjustable ring.

Rnd 1: Sc 2 in each st around. (16 sts)

Rnd 2: *Sc 3, sc 2 in next st; rep from * 3 more times. (20 sts)

Rnd 3: *Sc 4, sc 2 in next st; rep from * 3 more times. (24 sts)

Rnd 4: *Sc 5, sc 2 in next st; rep from * 3 more times. (28 sts)

Rnds 5-7: Sc 28.

Rnd 8: *Sc 5, sc2tog; rep from * 3 more times. (24 sts)

Rnd 9: *Sc 4, sc2tog; rep from * 3 more times. (20 sts)

Rnd 10: *Sc 3, sc2tog; rep from * 3 more times. (16 sts)

Rnd 11: Sc2tog 8 times. (8 sts)

Stuff pudding, fasten off yarn, close hole, and weave in end.

GLAZE

With ivory, make an 8-st adjustable ring.

Rnd 1: Sc 2 in each st around. (16 sts)

Rnd 2: *Sc 3, sc 2 in next st; rep from * 3 more times. (20 sts)

Rnd 3: *Sc 4, sc 2 in next st; rep from * 3 more times. (24 sts)

Rnd 4: *Sc 5, sc 2 in next st; rep from * 3 more times. (28 sts)

For the "drip" details, randomly alternate between chs of 3, 4, 5, or 6.

Rnd 5: *Sl st 1, ch 3/4/5/6, sc 2 in back ridge loop of 2nd ch from hook, sl st in remaining back ridge loops as well as the base of ch, sl st 1; rep from * 13 more times.

Place glaze on top of pudding and pin drips in place. For some additional variety "twist" some of the drips so their WS is facing out before pinning them down. Sew glaze and drips in place.

With tan yarn, apply random short sts over the pudding for texture.

FIGGY PUDDING *(continued)*

HOLLY LEAF (MAKE 2)

With green, loosely ch 6. Sl st in first st of ch to make a loop.

Rnd 1: Working in ch-6 sp (sl st 1, ch 2, sl st in base of ch 2) 7 times.

Sl st to fasten off yarn in ch-6 sp. Use leftover yarn tail to sew the hole closed in the middle of the leaf.

Attach holly leaves to top of pudding glaze. With invisible thread and a beading needle, attach a group of 3 red beads at the base of the holly leaves.

Attach hanging loop (page 18).

TO ADD A BIT OF FRAGRANT FUN TO YOUR CROCHETED BAKED GOODS, TRY DABBING A LITTLE FRAGRANCE OIL ONTO A SMALL PIECE OF STUFFING BEFORE ADDING IT TO YOUR ORNAMENT. YOU CAN FIND A WIDE VARIETY OF FRAGRANCE OILS FROM WWW.NATURESGARDENCANDLES.COM AND OTHER ONLINE RETAILERS.

GINGERBREAD KIDS

······ EASY • FINISHED SIZE: 1½" WIDE, 2½" TALL ······

⋗ MATERIALS ⋖

- Sock weight yarn in dark brown, ivory, and tan
- Hook size C (2.75 mm)
- Invisible or white thread
- Sewing needle
- White fabric puff paint (optional)
- Fine white glitter (optional)
- Tapestry needle
- Scissors
- (2) 10 mm jump rings

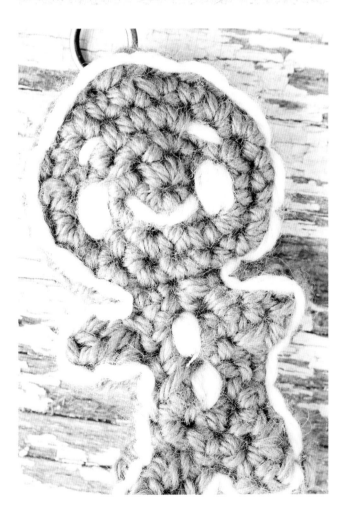

WITH PANTS (MAKE 2)

Head

With tan or dark brown, make a 6-st adjustable ring.

Rnd 1: Sc 2 in each st around.

Rnd 2: *Sc 1, sc 2 in next st; rep from * 5 more times. (18 sts)

Rnd 3: *Sc 2, sc 2 in next st; rep from * 5 more times. (24 sts)

Cont working body.

Body

Sl st in next st and ch 4.

Row 1: Working in back ridge loops, sc 3 in 2nd ch from hook, sc in back ridge loops of next 2 chs, sc in st at the base of ch-4, sl st 1 in rnd 3 of head, turn. (7 sts)

Row 2: Sk 1, sc 3, sc 2 in next 3 sts, sc in the front side of next 2 chs, sl st 1 in rnd 3 of head, turn. (12 sts)

Row 3: Ch 1, (hdc 1, dc 1, ch 2, sl st 1) in sl st, sl st 3, (sl st 1, ch 2 dc 1, ch 2, sl st 1) in next st, sl st 1, (sl st 1, ch 2 dc 1, ch 2, sl st 1) in next st, sl st 3, sk 1, (sl st 1, ch 2, dc 1, hdc 1) in next st, sl st in the corner where the head and neck meet, and fasten off yarn.

Hold WS of front and back pieces tog and whip stitch around outside edges.

WITH SKIRT (MAKE 2)

Head

With tan or dark brown, make a 6-st adjustable ring.

Rnd 1: Sc 2 in each st around. (12 sts)

Rnd 2: *Sc 1, sc 2 in next st; rep from * 5 more times. (18 sts)

Rnd 3: Sc 2, (sc 1, ch 3, sl st in back ridge loop of 3rd ch from hook, sc 1) in next st *sc 2, sc 2 in next st; rep from * 3 more times, (sc 1, ch 3, sl st in back ridge loop of 3rd ch from hook, sc 1) in next st, sc 2. (24 sts)

Cont working body.

GINGERBREAD KIDS *(continued)*

Body

Sl st in next st and ch 4.

Row 1: Working in back ridge loops, sc 3 in 2nd ch from hook, sc in back ridge loops of next 2 chs, sc in st at the base of ch-4, sl st 1 in rnd 3 of head, turn. (7 sts)

Row 2: Sk 1, sc 3, sc 2 in next 3 sts, sc in the front side of next 2 chs, sl st 1 in rnd 3 of head, turn. (12 sts)

Row 3: Ch 1, (hdc 1, dc 1, ch 2, sl st 1) in sl st, sl st 2, sc 1, (sc 1, ch 2, hdc 2) in next st, sc 1, (hdc 2, ch 2, sc 1) in next st, sc 1, sl st 2, sk 1, (sl st 1, ch 2, dc 1, hdc 1) in next st, sl st in the corner where the head and neck meet, and fasten off yarn.

Hold WS of front and back pieces tog and whip stitch around outside edges.

Gingerbread kids "iced" in puff paint and glitter.

DECORATING OPTIONS

1. With ivory yarn and white or invisible thread, couch a line of yarn around the outline of the cookie. Apply other embroidery details with long and short sts with a tapestry needle and yarn.

2. With white puff paint fabric, apply an "icing" to the cookie. While still wet, sprinkle with white glitter for a sanding sugar effect and set aside to dry completely.

Attach hanging loop (page 18).

OOPS! IF YOU MAKE A MISTAKE WHEN APPLYING YOUR PUFF PAINT, GENTLY RINSE OFF THE PAINT WHILE IT IS STILL WET, THEN PRESS YOUR WORK IN BETWEEN PAPER TOWELS TO DRAW OUT THE EXTRA WATER. FINALLY, GIVE YOUR COOKIE A BLAST OF HOT AIR FROM A BLOW DRYER AND YOU SHOULD BE ALL SET TO TRY FROSTING WITH PUFF PAINT AGAIN!

GINGERBREAD HOUSE

······ INTERMEDIATE • FINISHED SIZE - 2½" WIDE/DEEP, 2¾" TALL ······

⇌ MATERIALS ⇌

- Sock weight yarn in green, dark brown, red, and white
- Hook size C (2.75 mm)
- Invisible or white thread
- (8) 7 mm red beads
- (1) 6 mm gold bead
- (1) 4 mm white bead
- Sewing needle
- Tapestry needle
- Scissors
- (1) 10 mm jump ring

HOUSE BASE

In dark brown, loosely ch 5.

Rnd 1: Starting in 2nd ch from hook and working in back ridge loops, sc 3, sc 3 back ridge loop of next ch. Rotate ch so front side of ch is facing up. Starting in front side of the next ch, sc 2, sc 2 in front side of next ch. (14 sts)

Rnd 2: Sc 3 in next st, sc 2, sc 3 in next st, sc 1, sc 3 in next st, sc 2, sc 3 in next st, sc 1. (18 sts)

Rnd 3: Sc 1, sc 3 in next st, sc 4, sc 3 in next st, sc 3, sc 3 in next st, sc 4, sc 3 in next st, sc 2. (26 sts)

Rnd 4: Sc 2, sc 3 in next st, sc 6, sc 3 in next st, sc 5, sc 3 in next st, sc 6, sc 3 in next st, sc 3. (26 sts)

Cont working walls:

TALL WALL #1

Row 1: Sl st 3, BPsc 10, turn. (10 sts)

Rows 2-5: Ch 1, sc 10, turn. (10 sts)

Row 6: Ch 1, sc2tog, sc 6, sc2tog, turn. (8 sts)

Row 7: Ch 1, sc 8, turn. (8 sts)

Row 8: Ch 1, sc2tog, sc 4, sc2tog, turn. (6 sts)

Row 9: Ch 1, sc 6, turn. (6 sts)

Row 10: Ch 1, sc2tog, sc 2, sc2tog, turn. (4 sts)

Row 11: Ch 1, sc 4, turn. (4 sts)

Row 12: Ch 1, sc2tog 2 times, turn. (2 sts)

Row 13: Ch 1, sc 2, turn. (2 sts)

Row 14: Ch 1, sc2tog, turn. (1 st)

Row 15: Ch 1, sl st 1. (1 st)

Sl st 14 down side of wall. Cont working in sts from rnd 4 starting with st at the base of the wall edge.

SHORT WALL #1

Row 1: BPsc 7.

Rows 2-5: Ch 1, sc 7, turn. (7 sts)

Sl st 5 down side of wall. Cont working in sts from rnd 4 starting with st at the base of the wall edge.

GINGERBREAD HOUSE *(continued)*

TALL WALL #2

Row 1: BPsc 10, turn. (10 sts)

Cont Rows 2-14 as written for tall wall #1.

Sl st 14 down side of wall. Cont working in sts from rnd 4 starting with st at the base of the wall edge.

SHORT WALL #2

Repeat short wall #1 and fasten off yarn. With dark brown, sew the wall side edges tog with a whip stitch.

CANDY CANE SIDE POST (MAKE 4)

In white, loosely ch 7. Starting in 2nd ch from hook and working in back ridge loops, sl st 6. Fasten off yarn.

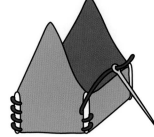

Sew side posts over the wall corners of the house base. Thread a tapestry needle with red yarn and whip stitch the yarn around each side post to create the candy cane stripes.

ROOF PANEL (MAKE 2)

In dark brown, loosely ch 13.

Row 1: Starting in 2nd ch from hook and working in back ridge loops, sc 12, turn. (12 sts)

Row 2: Ch 1. In bl, *sl st 1, (sl st 1, ch 3) in next st, sl st 2; to last 3 sts, sl st 1, (sl st 1, ch 3) in next st, sl st 1, turn.

Row 3: Ch 1, sl st 1, (sc 1, hdc 2, sc 1) in ch-3 sp, sk 1, sl st 2; to last 3 sts, sl st 1, (sc 1, hdc 2, sc 1) in ch-3 sp, sk 1, sl 1, turn.

Fold shingles away from you toward the shingled side of the work.

Row 4: Ch 1. Working in fls of row 2, sk ch 1, sc 12, turn. (12 sts)

Row 5: Ch 1, sc 12, turn.

Row 6: Ch 1. In bl, (sl st and ch 2, sl st) in same st *sl st 2, (sl st 1, ch 3) in next st, sl st 1; rep from * to last 3 sts, sl st 2, (sl st and ch 2, sl st) in same st, turn.

Row 7: Ch 1, (hdc 1, sc 1) in ch-2 sp, *sk 1, sl st 2, (sc 1, hdc 2, sc 1) in ch-3 sp; to last 3 sts, sk 1, sl st 2, (sc 1, hdc 1) in ch-2 sp, sl st 1, turn.

Fold shingles away from you toward the shingled side of the work.

Row 8: Ch 1. Working in fls of row 6, sc 12, turn. (12 sts)

Row 9: Ch 1, sc 12, turn.

Repeat rows 2-3.

Row 12: Ch 1. Working in fls of row 10, sc 12, turn. (12 sts)

Repeat rows 5-7.

Row 16: Ch 1. Working in fls of row 14, sc 12, turn. (12 sts)

Repeat rows 9, 2-3.

Row 20: Ch 1. Working in fls of row 18, sc 12, turn. (12 sts)

Repeat row 5.

Fasten off yarn.

WHITE EDGING DETAIL

Hold work with the round edges of the shingles pointed up.

White edge #1

Start on the right side of the first row of shingles at the top of your work (row 3).

(Sl st, ch 1) into first st of row 3, *sc 4, sc2tog; rep from * to last 5 sts, sc 4, sl st 1, and fasten off yarn on the side of the last shingle.

Work white edge #1 onto rows 11 and 19.

White edge #2

Start on the right side of the 2nd row of shingles from the top of your work (row 7).

(Sl st, ch 1, sc 1) into first st of row 7, sc 1, sc2tog, *sc 4, sc2tog; rep from * to last 5 sts, sc 4, sl st 1, and fasten off yarn on the side of the last shingle.

Work white edge #2 onto row 15.

Use a crochet hook to pull all the white yarn tails through to the back of the work so they can be tucked into the house when the roof panels are sewn onto the house base.

Using dark brown yarn, attach the roof panels by whip stitching the panel's side edges and bottom edge of row 1 to the front, back, and side edges of the house base. Leave the top ridge of the roof open and stuff house. Close roof seam and weave in ends.

SIDE EAVES

In white, loosely ch 26.

Row 1: Starting in 2nd ch from hook and working in back ridge loops, sc 25, ch 1, and turn. (25 sts)

Row 2: Sk ch 1, *sl st 1, (sl st 1, ch 3) in next st, sl st 1; rep from * to end.

Attach the flat edges of the side eaves to the sides of the roofline. As you attach the side eaves, you can also add a few stitches along the edge of the shingles to keep them from curling up.

ROOF RIDGE

In white, loosely ch 11.

Rnd 1: Starting in 2nd ch from hook and working in back ridge loops, sc 9, sc 4 in next st. Rotate ch so front side of ch is facing up. Starting in front side of the next ch, sc 8, sc 3 in front side of next ch. (24 sts)

Rnd 2: Sc 24.

Rnd 3: *Sl st 1, (sc 1, hdc 1) in next st, (hdc 1, sc 1) in next st; rep from * to end.

Fold long edges of the roof ridge together and apply a running st through rnd 2 to hold the folded shape. Sew ridge to the top of the roof. With invisible thread and a beading needle, sew eight 7-mm red beads to the ruffled parts of the ridge.

DOOR

In green, loosely ch 5.

Rnd 1: Starting in 2nd ch from hook and working in back ridge loops, sc 3, sc 3 in next st. Rotate ch so front side of ch is facing up. Starting in front side of the next ch, sc 2, sc 2 in front side of next ch. (10 sts)

Rnd 2: Sc 3 in next st, sc 2, (sc 2, ch 2, sc 1) in next st, sl st 1, (sc 1, ch 2, sc 2) in next st, sc 2, sc 3 in next st, sc 2 in next st, and fasten off yarn.

Sew door to front of house. Sew a 6-mm gold bead to the door for a door knob.

DOOR FRAME

In white, loosely ch 21, starting in 2nd ch from hook and working in back ridge loops, sl st 20. Fasten off yarn.

Sew door frame around sides and top of door. Thread a tapestry needle with red yarn and whip stitch the yarn around the door frame to create the candy cane stripes.

With white, apply a grouping of 6 lazy daisy sts in a flower pattern above the door and door frame. Apply a 4-mm white bead to the center of the flower.

Attach hanging loop (page 18).

CANDY CANE

······ EASY • FINISHED SIZE: 3" TALL, ½" WIDE ······

⇌ MATERIALS ⇌

- Sock weight yarn in red and white
- Hook size C (2.75 mm)
- ⅝" green ribbon
- Craft glue or needle and thread
- White pipe cleaner
- Tapestry needle
- Scissors
- (1) 10 mm jump ring

In white, make a 3-st adjustable ring.

Rnd 1: Sc 2 in each st around. (6 sts)

Rnd 2: In bl, sc 1, hdc 1, dc 1. Drop white loop from hook and leave loose. In red (sl st, ch 1, sc 1) in bl of next rnd 2 st. Cont to work in bl, hdc 1, dc 1. (6 sts)

Work the spiral: *Work red sc sts in the white sts until you reach the white loop. Drop the red loop from hook and leave loose. Pick up the white loop and work hdc sts in the red sts until you reach the red loop. Drop the white loop from hook and leave loose. Pick up the red loop; repeat from * until work measures 5" long.

Continue to work red sc sts in the white sts until you reach the white loop. Drop the red loop from hook and fasten off yarn. Fold a white pipe cleaner into a loop and twist ends around each other. Insert looped pipe cleaner into candy cane. Pick up the white loop. In bl, sc 6 and fasten off yarn.

Weave remaining white yarn tail through fls of last 6 sts and cinch to close hole. Weave in yarn tails and bend candy cane into final shape.

Tie ribbon bow around candy cane. To keep ribbon from fraying, dab a light coating of craft glue to the back of the ribbon ends.

Attach hanging loop (page 18).

HOT CHOCOLATE

······ EASY • FINISHED SIZE: 2⅜" TALL, 2" WIDE······

CUP

With red, make a 6-st adjustable ring.

Rnd 1: Sc 2 in each st around. (12 sts)

Rnd 2: *Sc 1, sc 2 in next st; rep from * 5 more times. (18 sts)

Rnd 3: *Sc 2, sc 2 in next st; rep from * 5 more times. (24 sts)

Rnd 4: BPsc 24.

Rnds 5-6: Sc 24.

Rnd 7: *Sc 6, sc2tog; rep from * 2 more times. (21 sts)

Rnds 8-10: Sc 21.

Rnd 11: *Sc 6, sc 2 in next st; rep from * 2 more times. (24 sts)

Rnd 12: Sc 24.

Rnd 13: *Sc 5, sc 2 in next st; rep from * 3 more times. (28 sts)

Rnds 14-15: Sc 28.

Rnd 16: *Sc 5, sc2tog; rep from * 3 more times. (24 sts)

Rnd 17: Sc 24.

Rnd 18: *Sc 6, sc2tog; rep from * 2 more times. (21 sts)

Rnds 19-21: Sc 21.

Rnd 22: *Sc 6, sc 2 in next st; rep from *2 more times. (24 sts)

Rnd 23: Sc 24. Fasten off yarn.

Fold rnd 23 down and into cup until it reaches the floor of the cup interior. Sew in place.

MATERIALS

- Sock weight yarn in dark brown, red, and white
- Hook size C (2.75 mm)
- Craft glue or needle and thread
- Tapestry needle
- Scissors
- (1) 10 mm jump ring

HOT CHOCOLATE *(continued)*

HANDLE

With red, make a 4-st adjustable ring.

Rnds 1-6: Sc 4.

Sew open edge of handle to upper half of cup side; curve handle and attach other end of handle to bottom half of cup side.

WHIPPED CREAM

With white, make a 6-st adjustable ring.

Rnd 1: Sc 2 in each st around. (12 sts)

Rnd 2: In bl, *sc 2, sc2tog; rep from * 2 more times. (9 sts)

Rnd 3: In bl, *sc 1, sc2tog; rep from * 2 more times. (6 sts)

Rnd 4: In bl, sc2tog 3 times. (3 sts)

Turn, ch 1, and sl st in each of the exposed fls that form a spiral from rnd 4 to rnd 1.

Attach bottom of whipped cream to the top of the hot chocolate.

With white, embroider a snowflake design to the outside of the mug.

Attach hanging loop (page 18).

HOT CHOCOLATE

With dark brown, make a 5-st adjustable ring.

Rnd 1: Sc 2 in each st around.

Rnd 2: *Sc 1, sc 2 in next st; rep from * 4 more times. (15 sts)

Rnd 3: *Sc 2, sc 2 in next st; rep from * 4 more times. (20 sts)

Rnd 4: BPsc 20.

Rnds 5-6: Sc 20.

Rnd 7: *Sc 3, sc2tog; rep from * 3 more times. (16 sts)

Rnds 8-10: Sc 16.

Rnd 11: *Sc 2, sc2tog; rep from * 3 more times. (12 sts)

Stuff hot chocolate.

Rnd 12: Sc2tog 6 times. (6 sts)

Fasten off yarn, close hole, and weave in yarn. Insert hot chocolate into cup and tack in place with a few sts of red.

FUN IN THE SNOW

WHEN THE
snow
STARTS FALLING, THESE
THREE COLD-LOVING
friends
CAN'T WAIT TO
bundle up
AND HEAD OUTSIDE FOR
SOME WINTERTIME
fun!

SNOWFLAKE

······ BEGINNER • FINISHED SIZE: 1¾" TALL/WIDE ·······

⇌ MATERIALS ⇌

- Sock weight yarn in light blue, medium blue, and white
- Hook size C (2.75 mm)
- Polyester fiberfill
- (36) 11/0 seed beads in white or light blue
- (1) 6 mm clear crystal bead
- Tapestry needle
- Invisible thread and beading needle
- Scissors
- (1) 10 mm jump ring

KEEP SL STS LOOSE TO MAKE THEM EASIER TO WORK IN.

SNOWFLAKE (MAKE 2)

In white, make a 6-st adjustable ring.

Rnd 1: (Sl st 1, ch 2, sl st 1) in each st around.

Rnd 2: *Sl st in next sl st, (sc 1, ch 2, sc 1) in ch-2 sp, sk next sl st, rep from * 5 more times.

Rnd 3: *Sl st in next sl st, sl st in next sc, (sc 1, ch 2, sc 1) in ch-2 sp, sl st in next sc; rep from * 5 more times.

Rnd 4: *Sl st in next 2 sl sts, sl st in next sc, (sc 1, ch 2, sc 1) in ch-2 sp, sl st in next sc, sl st in next sl st; rep from * 5 more times.

Fasten off yarn, leaving a long tail for sewing.

Hold WS of front and back pieces tog and whip stitch around edge of snowflakes and stuff before closing seams. Draw yarn back and forth through both layers of the snowflake in the center to sink the middle slightly and fasten off yarn.

Using light blue and medium blue and the diagram, apply long sts in a snowflake pattern to 1 side of the snowflake. With invisible thread, sew seed beads to the ends of the snowflake branches. Sew the crystal bead to the center of the snowflake.

Attach hanging loop (page 18).

SNOWMAN

······ BEGINNER • FINISHED SIZE: 3˝ TALL, 1½˝ WIDE ······

⚶ MATERIALS ⚶

- Sock weight yarn in black, dark brown, orange, and white
- Hook size C (2.75 mm)
- Craft glue or needle and thread
- Polyester fiberfill
- (2) 4 mm plastic eyes
- Tapestry needle
- Scissors
- Red felt
- (1) 10 mm jump ring

BODY AND HEAD

Using white, make an 8-st adjustable ring.

Rnd 1: Sc 2 in each st around. (16 sts)

Rnd 2: *Sc 1, sc 2 in next st; rep from * 7 more times. (24 sts)

Rnd 3: *Sc 2, sc 2 in next st; rep from * 7 more times. (32 sts)

Rnds 4-5: Sc 32.

Rnd 6: *Sc 2, sc2tog; rep from * 7 more times. (24 sts)

Rnd 7: Sc 24.

Rnd 8: *Sc 1, sc2tog; rep from * 7 more times. (16 sts)

Rnd 9: In fl, *sc 1, sc 2 in next st; rep from * 7 more times. (24 sts)

Rnd 10: Sc 24.

Rnd 11: *Sc 2, sc2tog; rep from * 5 more times. (18 sts)

Rnd 12: *Sc 1, sc2tog; rep from * 5 more times. (12 sts)

Stuff body firmly.

Rnd 13: In fl, *sc 2, sc 2 in next st; rep from * 3 more times. (16 sts)

Rnd 14: *Sc 3, sc 2 in next st; rep from * 3 more times. (20 sts)

Rnds 15-17: Sc 20.

Rnd 18: *Sc 3, sc2tog; rep from * 3 more times. (16 sts)

Rnd 19: *Sc 2, sc2tog; rep from * 3 more times. (12 sts)

Stuff head.

Rnd 20: Sc2tog 6 times.

Fasten off yarn and close hole at the top of the head.

With black yarn, apply 2 groupings of short satin sts to the middle and lower sections of the body for coal buttons.

SNOWMAN *(continued)*

HAT

Using black, make a 6-st adjustable ring.

Rnd 1: Sc 2 in each st around. (12 sts)

Rnd 2: In bl, *Sc 3, sc2tog; rep from * 1 more time. (10 sts)

Rnd 3: *Sc 2, sc2tog; rep from * 1 more time. (8 sts)

Rnds 4-5: Sc 8.

Rnd 6: In fl, sc 2 in each st around. (16 sts)

Rnd 7: Sl st 16.

Fasten off yarn.

Cut red felt into (1) ¼" by 2" strip. Glue or sew around hat just above the brim. Attach hat to top of head.

NOSE

Using orange, make a 3-st adjustable ring.

Rnd 1: Sc 2 in each st around. (6 sts)

Rnd 2: *Sc 1, sc2tog; rep from * 1 more time. (4 sts)

Fasten off yarn and close hole at tip of nose.

Attach rnd 1 of nose to center of face. Glue or sew on plastic eyes on either side of the carrot nose.

ARM (MAKE 2)

Using dark brown, loosely ch 7.

Starting in 2nd ch from hook and working in back ridge loops, sl st 2, *ch 3, starting in 2nd ch from hook and working in back ridge loops, sl st 3; rep from * 1 more time, sl st 4 to end of ch-7. Fasten off yarn.

Sew arms to shoulders of body.

FINISHING

Cut red felt into (1) ⅜" by 5½" strip. Bring the scarf around the neck and cross the tails (left side over right). Tuck the left tail under the right tail and draw it up and over the top edge of the scarf. Pull gently to tighten the knot and allow the left tail to hang down over the cross point. To keep the tail flat, tack it down with a dab of glue or sew in place if desired. Trim the scarf tails to preferred length and snip 3 small slits into each tail edge to create a fringe.

Attach hanging loop (page 18).

POLAR BEAR

······ EASY • FINISHED SIZE: 2½" TALL, 2¾" WIDE ······

⇌ MATERIALS ⇌

- Sock weight yarn in black and white
- Hook size C (2.75 mm)
- Polyester fiberfill
- (2) 4 mm plastic eyes
- Tapestry needle
- Scissors
- Craft glue or needle and thread
- Green felt
- (1) 10 mm jump ring

BODY

Using white, make an 6-st adjustable ring.

Rnd 1: Sc 2 in each sc around. (12 sts)

Rnd 2: *Sc 2, sc 2 in next sc; rep from * 3 more times. (16 sts)

Rnd 3: *Sc 3, sc 2 in next sc; rep from * 3 more times. (20 sts)

Rnd 4: *Sc 4, sc 2 in next sc; rep from * 3 more times. (24 sts)

Rnd 5: *Sc 4, sc2tog; rep from * 3 more times. (20 sts)

Rnd 6: Sc 20.

Rnd 7: *Sc 3, sc2tog; rep from * 3 more times. (16 sts)

Rnd 8: Sc 16.

Rnd 9: *Sc 2, sc2tog; rep from * 3 more times. (12 sts)

Stuff firmly. Fasten off yarn, leaving a long tail for sewing.

HEAD

In white, loosely ch 4.

Rnd 1: Starting in 2nd ch from hook and working in back ridge loops, sc 2, sc 5 back ridge loop of next ch. Rotate ch so front side of ch is facing up. Starting in front side of the next ch, sc 1, sc 4 in front side of next ch. (12 sts)

Rnd 2: Sc 2 in next st, sc 1, sc2 in next 5 sts, sc 1, sc 2 in next 4 sts. (22 sts)

Rnds 3-5: Sc 22.

Rnd 6: *Sc 9, sc2tog; rep from * 1 more time. (20 sts)

Rnd 7: Sc 20.

Rnd 8: *Sc 2, sc2tog; rep from * 4 more times. (15 sts)

Rnd 9: *Sc 1, sc2tog; rep from * 4 more times. (10 sts)

Fasten off yarn and stuff head. Flatten and close seam in a line with a mattress stitch at the top of the head.

Attach bottom of head to open end of body.

POLAR BEAR *(continued)*

MUZZLE

In white, make an 8-st adjustable ring.

Rnd 1: Sc 8.

Fasten off yarn.

Attach open edge of muzzle to lower half of face. Apply 4 satin sts in black for nose. Glue or sew 4 mm plastic eyes or beads to the face just above the muzzle. Using a single yarn ply from your black yarn or black embroidery thread, apply one short stitch above each eye for an eyebrow.

LEG (MAKE 4)

In white, make a 6-st adjustable ring.

Rnd 1: Sc 2 in each st around. (12 sts)

Rnd 2: In bl, sc 2, hdc 8, and sc 2. (12 sts)

Rnd 3: Sc 3, sc2tog 3 times, and sc 3. (9 sts)

Rnds 4-7: Sc 9.

Stuff leg lightly.

Rnd 8: *Sc 1, sc2tog; rep from * 2 more times. (6 sts)

Fasten off yarn, leaving a long tail. Flatten and close up the 6-st hole and weave in the end.

Sew the tops of the legs to the hips and shoulders of the bear. Sew the inside edges of the limbs to the body to secure the posed seated position. Using a single yarn ply from your black yarn or black embroidery thread, apply 3 short sts to the fronts of the paws to create toes.

TAIL

In white, make an 8-st adjustable ring.

Rnd 1: *Sc 2, sc2tog; rep from * 1 more time. (6 sts) Fasten off yarn.

Flatten the tail open edge and sew shut. Attach tail to back of body.

EAR (MAKE 2)

In white, make a 6-st adjustable ring. Sl st and fasten off yarn. Sew ears to the top corners of the head.

FINISHING

Cut green felt into (1) ⅜" by 5½" strip. Bring the scarf around the neck and cross the tails (left side over right). Tuck the left tail under the right tail and draw it up and over the top edge of the scarf. Pull gently to tighten the knot and allow the left tail to hang down over the cross point. To keep the tail flat, tack it down with a dab of glue or sew in place if desired. Trim the scarf tails to preferred length and snip 3 small slits into each tail edge to create a fringe.

Apply (1) 4" piece of white yarn to the top of the head using the fringe technique. Trim short and separate the yarn plys with a tapestry needle to create a bit of fuzz.

Attach hanging loop (page 18).

PENGUIN

······ EASY • FINISHED SIZE: 2¼" TALL, 1½" WIDE ······

MATERIALS

- Sock weight yarn in black, light blue, orange, and white
- Hook size C (2.75 mm)
- Tapestry needle
- Scissors
- Polyester fiberfill
- (2) 4 mm plastic eyes
- Craft glue
- Needle and black thread
- Lavender felt
- (1) 10 mm jump ring

BODY

When working the color changes in the body, carry/float the unused color on the WS of your work as you stitch with the contrasting color.

Using black make an 8-st adjustable ring.

Rnd 1: Sc 2 in each st around. (16 sts)

Rnd 2: *Sc 1, sc 2 in next st; rep from * 7 more times. (24 sts)

Row 3: In bl, sc 9, change to white, sc 6, change to black, sc 9, turn. (24 sts)

Rows 4-5: Ch 1, sc 9, change to white, sc 6, change to black, sc 9, turn. (24 sts)

Row 6: Ch 1, sc 2, sc2tog, sc 2, sc2tog, sc 1, change to white, sc 6, change to black, sc 1, sc2tog, sc 2, sc2tog, sc 2, turn. (20 sts)

Rows 7-10: Ch 1, sc 7, change to white, sc 6, change to black, sc 7, turn. (20 sts)

Row 11: Ch 1, sc 7, change to white, sc 2, change to black, sc 2, change to white, sc 2, change to black, sc 7. (20 sts)

Hold seam edges together and work across the gap to rejoin next st and work in the round.

Rnd 12: *Sc 2, sc2tog; rep from * 4 more times. (15 sts)

Rnd 13: *Sc 1, sc2tog; rep from * 4 more times. (10 sts)

Rnd 14: Sc2tog 5 times. (5 sts)

Stuff body firmly. Fasten off yarn and close hole at the top of the head.

Using black, sew up seam in the back of the body. Apply a ch st around the edge of the white area and accentuate the peak detail at the top of the face.

Glue or sew 4 mm sew-on plastic eyes to the face. Apply a short st of black thread above each eye for an eyebrow.

In orange, satin st a beak below the peak detail.

PENGUIN *(continued)*

WING (MAKE 2)

In black, loosely ch 4.

Rnd 1: Starting in 2nd ch from hook and working in back ridge loops, sc 2, sc 3 in back ridge loop of next ch. Rotate ch so front side of ch is facing up. Starting in front side of the next ch, sc 1, sc 4 in fls of next ch. (10 sts)

Fasten off yarn.

Sew the larger end of the wing to the shoulder of the penguin and tack down the tip of the wings with the leftover yarn tails.

HAT

In light blue, make a 6-st adjustable ring.

Rnd 1: Sc 2 in each st around. (12 sts)

Rnd 2: *Sc 2, sc 2 in next st; rep from * 3 more times. (16 sts)

Rnd 3: *Sc 3, sc 2 in next st; rep from * 3 more times. (20 sts)

Rnds 4-5: Sc 20.

Fasten off yarn.

Sew hat to top of the head. Sew or glue (1) ⅜" by 4" strip of lavender felt around the brim of the hat. With light blue yarn, apply spaced-out perpendicular sts over the felt strip for a ribbing detail.

Apply (3) 3" pieces of white yarn to the top of the hat using the fringe technique. Trim short and separate the yarn plys with a tapestry needle to create a bit of fuzz.

Attach loop for hanging (page 18).

BABY'S FIRST CHRISTMAS

Celebrate

AND COMMEMORATE

THE WONDER, JOY, AND

warmth

OF BABY'S FIRST

Christmas.

SLEEPY SHEEP

······ EASY • FINISHED SIZE: 1¼" TALL, 1½" WIDE, 2½" LONG ······

⊰ MATERIALS ⊱

- Sock weight yarn in dark blue and ivory
- Hook size C (2.75 mm)
- Craft glue or needle and thread
- Polyester fiberfill
- (8") ¼" ribbon (optional)
- Tapestry needle
- Scissors
- (1) 10 mm jump ring

BODY

In ivory, make a 6-st adjustable ring.

Rnd 1: In bl, sc 2 in each st around. (12 sts)

Rnd 2: In bl, *sc 1, sc 2 in next st; rep from * 5 more times. (18 sts)

Rnds 3-7: In bl, sc 18.

Rnd 8: *Sc 1, sc2tog; rep from * 5 more times. (12 sts)

Stuff body.

Rnd 9: Sc2tog 6 times. (6 sts).

Fasten off yarn and close hole.

HEAD

In dark blue, make an 8-st adjustable ring.

Rnd 1: Sl st 1, sc 2 in next 2 sts, hdc 2 in next 2 sts, sc 2 in next 2 sts, sl st 1. (14 sts)

Rnd 2: Sc 14.

Rnd 3: Sl st 1, sc2tog 6 times, sl st 1. (8 sts)

Rnd 4: Sc 8.

Change to ivory.

Rnd 5: FPsc 8.

Stuff head.

Rnd 6: *Sc 2, sc2tog; rep from * 1 more time. (6 sts)

Fasten off yarn, close hole, and weave in end.

With the hdc sts from rnd 1 facing front, sew the head to the front of the body. With ivory yarn, embroider a "Y" shape to the lower half of the face for a nose detail. For the closed eyes, thin out a strand of yarn by separating out 2 yarn plys and apply 2 curved short sts to the front of the face. With a full strand of ivory yarn, apply 2 short sts above the eyes for eyebrows.

SLEEPY SHEEP *(continued)*

LEG (MAKE 4)

In dark blue, make a 4-st adjustable ring.

Rnd 1: *Sc 1, sc 2 in next st; rep from * 1 more time. (6 sts)

Rnd 2: Sc 6.

Fasten off yarn.

Sew the open edges of the legs to the bottom of the body.

EAR (MAKE 2)

In dark blue, ch 4, sl st 1 in back ridge loop of 4th ch from hook, and fasten off yarn.

Sew fastened-off end of ears to the sides of the head.

WOOL DETAIL

With ivory, (sl st, ch 3, sl st in back ridge loop in 2nd ch from hook) in surface stitch to join yarn to surface of body. Repeat this pattern in a random and wiggly path over the surface of the body until the entire ivory area is covered (working around the head and legs). Apply same treatment to the ivory top part of the head if desired.

TAIL

With ivory, ch 4, and sl st 1 in back ridge loop of 4th ch from hook.

Working in ch-4 sp, sl st 1, sc 1, hdc 2, sc 1 sl st 1, and fasten off yarn.

Sew tail to back of body.

Tie a ribbon around the neck if desired. To keep ribbon from fraying, dab a light coating of craft glue to the back of the ribbon ends.

Attach hanging loop (page 18).

MITTEN MOUSE

EASY • FINISHED SIZE (WITH MOUSE): 3¼" TALL, 2" WIDE

FINISHED SIZE MITTEN: 2½" TALL, 2" WIDE

⇌ MATERIALS ⇌

- Sock weight yarn in black, grey, ivory, and pink
- Hook size C (2.75 mm)
- Craft glue or needle and thread
- Polyester fiberfill
- (3) 4 mm plastic eyes
- (8") ¼" ribbon
- Tapestry needle
- Scissors
- (1) 10 mm jump ring

TO MAKE THE MITTEN WITHOUT A MOUSE AS SHOWN ON PAGE 19, YOU WILL NEED SOCK WEIGHT YARN IN IVORY AND DARK GREY.

MITTEN

In ivory, loosely ch 20; sl st in first ch to make a loop. Ch 2.

Rnd 1: Working in back ridge loops of ch-20, dc 20. (20 sts)

Rnd 2: Sl st 1 in top of ch-2 at beg of rnd 1; FPsc 20. (20 sts)

Rnd 3: BPsc 20.

Rnd 4: Sc 20.

Rnd 5: *Sc 9, sc 2 in next st; rep from * 1 more time. (22 sts)

Rnd 6: *Sc 10, sc 2 in next st; rep from * 1 more time. (24 sts)

Rnd 7: *Sc 5, sc 2 in next st; rep from * 3 more times. (28 sts)

Rnd 8: (Mitten thumb opening) (Sc 4, sc 2 in next st) 2 times, sk 8, (sc 2 in next st, sc 4) 2 times. (24 sts)

Rnd 9: Sc 11, sc 2 in next 2 sts, sc 11. (26 sts)

Rnd 10: Sc 12, sc 2 in next 2 sts, sc 12. (28 sts)

Rnd 11: *Sc 5, sc2tog; rep from * 3 more times. (24 sts)

Rnd 12: *Sc 4, sc2tog; rep from * 3 more times. (20 sts)

Rnd 13: Sc2tog 10 times. (10 sts)

Rnd 14: Sc2tog 5 times. (5 sts)

Fasten off yarn and close hole.

MITTEN THUMB

Rnd 1: In ivory, (sl st 1, ch 1, sc 1) in one of the mitten thumb opening sts from rnd 7 (counts as first sc). Cont to work 1 sc in each of the remaining 7 sts around the inside of the thumb opening. (8 sts)

Rnd 2: *Sc 2, sc2tog; rep from * 1 more time. (6 sts)

Fasten off yarn and close hole.

TIP #1: THIS LITTLE BABY MOUSE WILL ALSO FIT IN THE STOCKING FROM PAGE 38!

TIP #2: A PAIR OF MITTENS WITH INITIALS EMBROIDERED ON THEM CAN MAKE A CUTE ORNAMENT TO CELEBRATE A FIRST CHRISTMAS TOGETHER.

MITTEN MOUSE *(continued)*

MOUSE BODY

With grey, make a 6-st adjustable ring.

Rnd 1: Sc 2 in each st around. (12 sts)

Rnd 2: *Sc 2, sc 2 in next st; rep from 3 more times. (16 sts)

Rnd 3: *Sc 2, sc2tog; rep from * 3 more times. (12 sts)

Rnd 4: *Sc 1, sc2tog; rep from * 3 more times. (8 sts)

Rnd 5: Sc 8.

Lightly stuff body.

Rnd 6: Sc2tog 4 times. (4 sts)

Fasten off yarn, close hole, and weave in end.

MOUSE HEAD

With grey, make a 6-st adjustable ring.

Rnd 1: Sc 2 in each st around. (12 sts)

Rnd 2: *Sc 2, sc 2 in next st; rep from 3 more times. (16 sts)

Rnd 3: *Sc 2, sc2tog; rep from * 3 more times. (12 sts)

Rnd 4: *Sc 1, sc2tog; rep from * 3 more times. (8 sts)

Stuff head.

Rnd 5: *Sc 2, sc2tog; rep from * 1 more time. (6 sts)

Fasten off yarn, close hole, and weave in end.

Sew the head to the tapered end of the body. Tilt the head down and tack the chin of the mouse to the front of the body with a few sts to hold the pose in place.

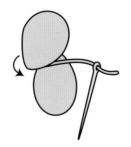

MOUSE EAR (MAKE 2)

With grey, make a 6-st adjustable ring and turn. Do not join ring.

Rnd 1: Ch 1, sl st 1, sc 2 in next 4 sts, sl st 1, and fasten off yarn.

Sew the straight edges of the ears to the sides of the head.

Glue or sew 4 mm plastic eyes or beads to the face 2 rnds back from the tip of the muzzle. Glue or sew 4 mm plastic eye to the front of the head (just above the tip of the muzzle) for a nose. Using a single yarn ply from your black yarn or black embroidery thread, apply 1 short st above each eye for an eyebrow.

MOUSE ARM (MAKE 2)

In grey, loosely ch 5.

Working in back ridge loops of ch, sc 2 in 2nd ch from hook, sl st 3, and fasten off yarn.

Attach fastened off ends to the shoulders of the mouse body.

FINISHING

Place mouse in the mitten so the head and shoulders are just above the top edge of the mitten cuff. With ivory, apply a few sts through the cuff and mouse body to hold the mouse in place.

With grey, pose and secure the hands to the mitten cuff with a st or two, then draw the leftover grey yarn tails up though the top of the head. Trim the grey yarn short and rub the yarn between your fingers for a bit of fuzzy mouse hair.

With pink, embroider a snowflake design on the front of the mitten with long and short sts and French knots.

Thread ¼" ribbon onto a tapestry needle and draw the ribbon through the dc stitch posts above rnd 2 of the mitten in a running st pattern with the ribbon tails beginning and ending at the front of the mitten. Tie the ribbon tails together in a square knot and then a bow.

To keep ribbon from fraying, dab a light coating of craft glue to the back of the ribbon ends.

Attach hanging loop (page 18).

BABY SHOES

······ EASY • FINISHED SIZE: 1" TALL, 2⅛" WIDE ······

⇾ MATERIALS ⇽

- Sock weight yarn in blue
- Hook size C (2.75 mm)
- (17") ¼" ivory ribbon
- (2) 6 mm ivory-colored pearls
- Tapestry needle
- Sewing needle and invisible thread
- Scissors
- (1) 10 mm jump ring

SHOE (MAKE 1 RIGHT AND 1 LEFT)

With blue, loosely ch 7.

Rnd 1: Starting in 2nd ch from hook and working in back ridge loops, sc 5, sc 5 back ridge loop of next ch. Rotate ch so front side of ch is facing up. Starting in front side of the next ch, sc 4, sc 2 in front side of next ch. (16 sts)

Rnd 2: Sc 2 in next st, sc 4, hdc 2 in next 5 sts, sc 4, sc 2 in next 2 sts. (24 sts)

Rnd 3: Sc 2 in next 2 sts, sc 4, sc 2 in next 10 sts, sc 4, sc 2 in next 4 sts. (40 sts)

Rnd 4: BPsc 40.

Rnd 5: Sc 5, sc2tog, sc 3, (hdc2tog, hdc 2) 2 times, (hdc 2, hdc2tog) 2 times, sc 3, sc2tog, sc 9. (34 sts)

Rnd 6: Sc 4, sc2tog, sc 2, sc2tog, hdc 4, hdc2tog, hdc 4, sc2tog, sc 2, sc2tog, sc 8. (28 sts)

Rnd 7: Sc 6, hdc2tog, hdc 8, hdc2tog, sc 6, sc2tog 2 times. (24 sts)

RIGHT SHOE STRAP

Rnd 8: Sc 4, sc2tog, ch 8, working in back ridge loops of ch 8, sc 2 in 2nd ch from hook, sc 6, sl st in st at base of ch-8, sc2tog 5 times, sc2tog, sc 6.

Fasten off yarn, leaving a long tail for sewing.

LEFT SHOE STRAP

Rnd 8: Sc 6, sc2tog, sc2tog 5 times, ch 8, working in back ridge loops of ch 8, sc 2 in 2nd ch from hook, sc 6, sl st in st at base of ch-8, sc2tog, sc 4.

Fasten off yarn, leaving a long tail for sewing.

FINISHING

Weave the leftover yarn tail in the back of the shoe through the inside edge of the shoe interior until you reach the point where the strap will overlap with the side of the shoe. Use the yarn tail to sew the end of the strap in place. Weave in remaining yarn ends.

Use a sewing needle and invisible thread to attach a 6 mm pearl to the end of the straps for a button detail.

BABY SHOES *(continued)*

Cut (1) 5" piece of ivory ribbon. Draw 1 end of the ribbon through the back of 1 shoe and tie a knot to keep the ribbon from pulling out. Apply a bit of glue to the knot and inside of shoe to fully secure ribbon if desired. Slip a jump ring/hanging loop onto the ribbon and repeat the process on the other shoe so both shoes are suspended on the ribbon.

Cut (2) 6" pieces of ribbon and tie bows to the back of the shoes directly in front of the hanging ribbons. To keep ribbons from fraying, dab a light coating of craft glue to the back of the ribbon ends.

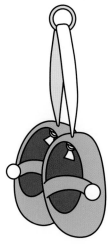

AN INVISIBLE HDC2TOG IS WORKED IN A SIMILAR WAY TO THE INVISIBLE SC2TOG (PAGE 13). TO BEGIN, YO AND THEN SLIP HOOK UNDER THE FLS OF THE NEXT 2 STS. YO AND DRAW THE HOOK THROUGH THE 2 FLS (YOU WILL HAVE 3 LOOPS ON YOUR HOOK). YO AND PULL THE HOOK THROUGH ALL 3 LOOPS TO COMPLETE THE HDC2TOG INVISIBLE DECREASE.

TEDDY HEART

······ EASY • FINISHED SIZE: 2¼" TALL, 1¾" WIDE ·······

⇌ MATERIALS ⇌

- Sock weight yarn in black, dark pink, ivory, and tan
- Hook size C (2.75 mm)
- Polyester fiberfill
- Tapestry needle
- (15–16) 11/0 purple seed beads
- Invisible thread and beading needle
- (3) 4 mm plastic eyes
- Scissors
- (1) 10 mm jump ring

BODY

In tan, make a 6-st adjustable ring.

Rnd 1: Sc 2 in each st around. (12 sts)

Rnd 2: *Sc 1, sc 2 in next st; rep from * 5 more times. (18 sts)

Rnd 3: Sc 18.

Rnd 4: *Sc 7, sc2tog; rep from * 1 more time. (16 sts)

Rnd 5: *Sc 6, sc2tog; rep from * 1 more time. (14 sts)

Rnd 6: *Sc 5, sc2tog; rep from * 1 more time. (12 sts)

Rnd 7: *Sc 1, sc2tog; rep from * 3 more times. (8 sts)

Fasten off yarn and stuff body. Leave neck edge open.

HEAD

In tan, loosely ch 4.

Rnd 1: Starting in 2nd ch from hook and working in back ridge loops, sc 2, sc 5 back ridge loop of next ch. Rotate ch so front side of ch is facing up. Starting in front side of the next ch, sc 1, sc 4 in front side of next ch. (12 sts)

Rnd 2: Sc 2 in next st, sc 1, sc2 in next 5 sts, sc 1, sc 2 in next 4 sts. (22 sts)

Rnd 3: Sc 22.

Rnd 4: *Sc 9, sc2tog; rep from * 1 more time. (20 sts)

Rnd 5-6: Sc 20.

Rnd 7: *Sc 2, sc2tog; rep from * 4 more times. (15 sts)

Rnd 8: *Sc 1, sc2tog; rep from * 4 more times. (10 sts)

Fasten off yarn and stuff head. Close seam in a straight line with a mattress stitch at the bottom of the head.

Attach head to open end of body. Secure yarn and draw leftover yarn tail up through the top of the head. Trim tails short for a bit of hair and soften the yarn plys with by separating them with your fingers.

TEDDY HEART *(continued)*

MUZZLE

In ivory, make an 6-st adjustable ring.

Rnd 1: Sc 6.

Fasten off yarn.

Attach open edge of muzzle to lower half of face. Glue or sew 2 4-mm plastic eyes or beads to the face just above the muzzle. Apply a 3rd 4-mm eye to the tip of the muzzle for a nose. Using a single yarn ply from your black yarn or black embroidery thread, apply 1 short st above each eye for an eyebrow.

EAR (MAKE 2)

In tan, make a 6-st adjustable ring. Sl st and fasten off yarn.

Sew ears to the top corners of the head.

PAW (MAKE 4)

In tan, make a 6-st adjustable ring.

Rnds 1-2: Sc 6.

Rnd 3: Sc 2, sc2tog, sc 2. (5 sts)

Rnd 4: Sc 5.

Fasten off yarn. Flatten seam and sew shut. Sew paws to shoulders and hips of body.

TAIL

In tan, make a 6-st adjustable ring.

Rnd 1: *Sc 1, sc2tog; rep from * 1 more time. (4 sts)

Fasten off yarn.

Sew open edge of tail to back of body.

HEART (MAKE 2)

With dark pink, make an 8-st adjustable ring.

Rnd 1: Sl st 1, (sc 1, hdc 3) in next st, sc 2, sc 3 in next st, sc 2, (hdc 3, sc 1) in next st. (15 sts)

Rnd 2: Sl st 1, sc 1, hdc 2 in next 3 sts, sc 2 in next 2 sts, sc 1, (sc 1, hdc 1, sc 1) in next st, sc 1, sc 2 in next 2 sts, hdc 2 in next 3 sts, sc 1. (28 sts).

Fasten off yarn, leaving a long tail for sewing.

FINISHING

Match up the front and back of the hearts with the WS tog. Sew edges tog using a whip stitch.

With ivory yarn, customize the heart with a date, name, or initials.

With tan yarn, secure the back layer of the heart to the teddy bear body. Run the tan yarn up through the limbs to secure the paws around the edges of the heart.

With invisible thread and a beading needle, sew purple seed beads around the edge of the heart.

Attach hanging loop (page 18).

WOODLAND FRIENDS

these cute *forest pals* are ready for christmas with their *warm* and toasty *scarves.*

OWL

······ EASY • FINISHED SIZE: 2" TALL, 1½" WIDE ······

⇌ MATERIALS ⇌

- Sock weight yarn in dark brown, tan, and yellow
- Hook size C (2.75 mm)
- Tapestry needle
- Scissors
- Reddish-brown felt
- Green felt
- Polyester fiberfill
- (2) 4 mm plastic eyes
- 2" twig
- Craft glue or needle and thread
- (1) 10 mm jump ring

BODY

When working the color changes in the body, carry/float the unused color on the WS of your work as you stitch with the contrasting color.

Using dark brown, make an 8-st adjustable ring.

Rnd 1: Sc 2 in each st around. (16 sts)

Rnd 2: *Sc 1, sc 2 in next st; rep from * 7 more times. (24 sts)

Row 3: Sc 9, change to tan, sc 6, change to dark brown, sc 9, turn. (24 sts)

Row 4: Ch 1, sc 2, sc2tog, sc 1, sc2tog, sc 1, change to tan, sc 8, change to dark brown, sc 1, sc2tog, sc 1, sc2tog, sc 2, turn. (20 sts)

Rows 5-7: Ch 1, sc 6, change to tan, sc 8, change to dark brown, sc 6, turn. (20 sts)

Row 8: Ch 1, sc 3, sc2tog, sc 1, change to tan, sc 8, change to dark brown, sc 1, sc2tog, sc 3, turn. (18 sts)

Row 9: Ch 1, sc 3, sc 2 in next st, sc 1, change to tan, sc 8, change to dark brown, sc 1, sc 2 in next st, sc 3, turn. (20 sts)

Row 10: Ch 1, sc 2, sc 2 in next st, sc 1, sc 2 in next st, sc 1, change to tan, sc 8, change to dark brown, sc 1, sc 2 in next st, sc 1, sc 2 in next st, sc 2, turn. (24 sts)

Row 11: Ch 1, sc 8, change to tan, sc 8, change to dark brown, sc 8. (24 sts)

Hold seam edges together and work across the gap to rejoin next st and work in the round.

Rnd 12: Sc 2, sc2tog, sc 1, sc2tog, sc 1, change to tan, sc 3, change to dark brown, sc 2, change to tan, sc 3, change to dark brown, sc 1, sc2tog, sc 1, sc2tog, sc 2. (20 sts)

Rnd 13: Sc 1, sc2tog, sc 1, sc2tog, sc 8, sc2tog, sc 1, sc2tog, sc 1.(16 sts)

Rnd 14: *Sc 2, sc2tog; rep from * 3 more times. (12 sts)

Fasten off yarn.

Close seam in the back of the body with a whip stitch. Stuff body. Close the seam along top of head in a straight line.

OWL *(continued)*

TUFT DETAILS

In dark brown and working in one of the corners at the top of the head, (sl st 1, ch 1, sc 1, ch 1) in surface st. Cut yarn and pull the yarn tail through the last ch 1. Trim loose ends short and separate yarn plys with fingers. Weave in remaining yarn tail and repeat in opposite corner of head.

In dark brown, apply a ch st around the edge of the tan area and accentuate the peak detail at the top of the face.

BEAK (MAKE 2)

In yellow, make a 3-st adjustable ring. Do not join ring. Cut yarn and pull yarn tail out through last st to secure.

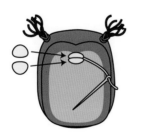

Stack the half-circle beak pieces and place the flat edges against the face directly under the brown "peak" detail and sew in place.

Cut out (2) ⅜" circles of reddish-brown felt and clip a small slit in the middle of the circles. Insert the post of the 4 mm plastic eyes into the circles. Apply glue to the back of the circle and eye post before applying them to the face on either side of the beak.

WING (MAKE 2)

In dark brown, loosely ch 5.

Rnd 1: Starting in 2nd ch from hook and working in back ridge loops, sl st 1, sc 2, and hdc 5 in back ridge loop of next ch. Rotate ch so front side of ch is facing up. Starting in front side of the next ch, sc 2, sl st 1, and fasten off yarn. (16 sts)

Sew the larger end of the wings to the shoulders of the owl.

TAIL

In dark brown, make a 6-st adjustable ring. Do not join ring.

Row 1: Ch 1, sc 1, hdc 2 in next 4 sts, sc 1, turn. (10 sts)

Row 2: Ch 1, sl st 1 (ch 3, sl st 1) 9 more times.

Fasten off yarn.

Sew the straight edge and corners of the tail to the back of the body around rnd 3.

Double up yellow yarn on a tapestry needle. Hold a small 2" long stick against the bottom of the owl and loop the yarn around the stick 3 to 4 times, catching the underside of the owl as you sew to create a foot. Repeat 1 more time to create the other foot.

Cut green felt into (1) ⅜" by 8½" strip. Bring the scarf around the neck and over the shoulders. Cross the scarf tails left side over right. Tuck the left tail under the right tail and draw it up and over the top edge of the scarf. Pull gently to tighten the knot and allow the left tail to hang down over the cross point. To keep the tail flat, tack it down with a dab of glue or sew in place if desired. Trim the scarf tails to preferred length and snip 3 small slits into each tail edge to create a fringe.

Attach hanging loop (page 18).

FOX

······· INTERMEDIATE • FINISHED SIZE: 2½" TALL, 1½" WIDE ·······

⇒ MATERIALS ⇐

- Sock weight yarn in black, ivory, and orange
- Hook size C (2.75 mm)
- Tapestry needle
- Scissors
- Green felt
- Polyester fiberfill
- (2) 4 mm plastic eyes
- Craft glue or needle and thread
- (1) 10 mm jump ring

HEAD BOTTOM

With ivory, make an 8-st adjustable ring.

Rnd 1: Sc 2 in each st around. (16 sts)

Rnd 2: (Muzzle opening) (Sc 2, sc 2 in next st) 2 times, ch 4, sk 4, (sc 2 in next st, sc 2) 2 times. (20 sts)

Rnd 3: Sc 8, sc in each st of ch-4, and sc 8. (20 sts)

Rnd 4: *Sc 4, sc2tog, sc 4; rep from * 1 more time. (18 sts)

Rnd 5: Sc 18.

Rnd 6: *Sc 1, sc2tog; rep from * 5 more times. (12 sts)

Rnd 7: Sc2tog 6 times. (6 sts)

Stuff head.

MUZZLE DETAIL

Rnd 1: In ivory, (sl st 1, ch 1 sc 1) in one of the muzzle opening sts (counts as first sc). Cont to work 1 sc in each of the remaining 7 sts around the inside of the muzzle opening. (8 sts)

Rnd 2: *Sc 1, sc2tog, sc 1; rep from * 1 more time. (6 sts)

Fasten off yarn, leaving a long tail. Lightly stuff muzzle and close hole. Use leftover yarn tail to patch any holes in the sides of the muzzle.

HEAD TOP

In orange, make an 8-st adjustable ring.

Rnd 1: Sc 2 in each st around. (16 sts)

Rnd 2: *Sc 1, sc 2 in next st; rep from * 7 more times. (24 sts)

Rnd 3: Sc 24.

Rnd 4: (Sc 1, sc2tog) 2 times, hdc 2, sc 1, sl st 2, sc 1, ch 5, starting in 2nd ch from hook and working in back ridge loops of ch-5, sl st 3, sc 1, working in rnd 3 sts, sc 1, sl st 2, sc 1, hdc 2 (sc2tog, sc 1) 2 times.

Place head top onto head bottom with ch-5 lined up with the muzzle. Sew ch-5 down to the bridge and tip of the muzzle, then sew edge of head top down to head bottom.

FOX *(continued)*

Glue or sew on 4 mm plastic eyes. Using a single yarn ply from your black yarn or black embroidery thread, apply 1 short st above each eye for an eyebrow.

Cut (6) 3" pieces of ivory yarn. Apply 3 fringe knots to the edge of each cheek. Trim short and separate and soften yarn plys with fingers.

NOSE

In black, make a 3-st adjustable ring. Do not join. Cut yarn and pull yarn tail out through last st to secure.

With the rounded edge of the nose pointed down, sew nose to tip of muzzle (overlapping the end of the orange ch-5).

EAR (MAKE 2)

In orange, make a 5-st adjustable ring and turn. Do not join.

Row 1: Ch 1, sl st 2, ch 2, hdc 2, ch 2, sl st in back ridge loop of 2nd ch from hook, ch 2, sl st 2, and fasten off yarn.

Sew flat edges of ears to the top of the head. Draw 2 leftover yarn tails from the ears up and out through the top of the head for a hair fringe. Trim short and soften the yarn plys with your fingers.

BODY

When working the color changes in the body, carry/float the unused color on the WS of your work as you stitch with the contrasting color.

In orange, make a 6-st adjustable ring.

Rnd 1: Sc 2 in each st around. (12 sts)

Row 2: Sc 4, change to ivory, sc 4, change to orange, sc 4, turn. (12 sts)

Rows 3-4: Ch 1, sc 3, change to ivory, sc 6, change to orange, sc 3, turn. (12 sts)

Row 5: Ch 1, sc 3, change to ivory, sc2tog, sc 2, sc2tog, change to orange, sc 3, turn. (10 sts)

Rows 6-7: Ch 1, sc 3, change to ivory, sc 4, change to orange, sc 3, turn. (10 sts)

Row 8: Ch 1, sc 3, change to ivory, sc2tog 2 times, change to orange, sc 3. (8 sts)

Hold seam edges together and work across the gap to rejoin next st and work in the round.

Rnd 9: *Sc 1, sc2tog, sc 1; rep from * 1 more time. (6 sts)

Fasten off yarn.

Stuff body and close seam in the back of the body with a whip stitch.

In orange, apply a ch st around the edge of the ivory area to clean up the edge.

Sew the bottom of the head to the open edge of the neck.

BACK LEG (MAKE 2)

Starting with black, make a 6-st adjustable ring.

Rnd 1: Sl st 1, sc 1, hdc 2, sc 1, sl st 1. (6 sts)

Rnd 2: Sc 1, sc2tog 2 times, sc 1. (4 sts)

Rnd 3: Sc 4.

FOX *(continued)*

Change to orange.

Rnd 4: Sc 4.

Rnd 5: *Sc 1, sc 2 in next st; rep from * 1 more time. (6 sts)

Rnd 6: *Sc 1, sc 2 in next st; rep from * 2 more times. (9 sts)

Rnd 7: *Sc 2, sc 2 in next st; rep from * 2 more times. (12 sts)

Rnd 8: Sc2tog 6 times. (6 sts)

Do not stuff leg. Fasten off yarn and close hole.

Fold the lower leg and upper leg together. Hold the shaping in place with a few sts. Sew the orange portion of the legs to the hips of the body.

FRONT LEG (MAKE 2)

Starting with black, make a 6-st adjustable ring.

Rnd 1: Sl st 1, sc 1, hdc 2, sc 1, sl st 1. (6 sts)

Rnd 2: Sc 1, sc2tog 2 times, sc 1. (4 sts)

Rnd 3: Sc 4.

Change to orange.

Rnds 4-7: Sc 4.

Fasten off yarn and close hole at the top of the leg.

Sew top of the leg to the shoulder of the body. Sew the inside edges of the legs to the body to keep them in place.

TAIL

Starting with orange, make a 3-st adjustable ring.

Rnd 1: Sc 3.

Rnd 2: Sc 2 in each st around. (6 sts)

Rnd 3: Sc 6.

Rnd 4: *Sc 2, sc 2 in next st; rep from * 1 more time. (8 sts)

Rnd 5: Sc 8.

Rnd 6: *Sc 3, sc 2 in next st; rep from * 1 more time. (10 sts)

Change to ivory.

Rnd 7: *Sc 4, sc 2 in next st; rep from * 1 more time. (12 sts)

Rnd 8: *Sc 4, sc2tog; rep from * 1 more time. (10 sts)

Rnd 9: *Sc 3, sc2tog; rep from * 1 more time. (8 sts)

Stuff tail.

Rnd 10: *Sc 2, sc2tog; rep from * 1 more time. (6 sts)

Fasten off yarn and close hole.

Attach orange end of tail to the bottom of the body. Pose tail and tack in place to the body with a few sts.

Cut green felt into (1) ⅜" by 6½" strip. Bring the scarf around the neck and over the shoulders. Cross the scarf tails left side over right. Tuck the left tail under the right tail and draw it up and over the top edge of the scarf. Pull gently to tighten the knot and allow the left tail to hang down over the cross point. To keep the tail flat, tack it down with a dab of glue or sew in place if desired. Trim the scarf tails to preferred length and snip 3 small slits into each tail edge to create a fringe.

Attach hanging loop (page 18).

MOOSE

······ INTERMEDIATE • FINISHED SIZE (WITH ANTLERS): 3½" TALL, 2½" LONG, 2" WIDE ······

⤙ MATERIALS ⤚

- Sock weight yarn in black, dark brown, and tan
- Hook size C (2.75 mm)
- Tapestry needle
- Scissors
- Polyester fiberfill
- (2) 4 mm plastic eyes
- Green felt
- Craft glue or needle and thread
- (1) 10 mm jump ring

HEAD AND MUZZLE

In dark brown, make a 6-st adjustable ring.

Rnd 1: Sc 2 in each st around. (12 sts)

Rnd 2: *Sc 2, sc 2 in next st; rep from * 3 more times. (16 sts)

Rnds 3-5: Sc 16.

Rnd 6: *Sc 2, sc2tog; rep from * 3 more times. (12 sts)

Stuff head.

Rnd 7: *Sc 1, sc2tog; rep from * 3 more times. (8 sts)

Rnd 8: Sc 2 in each st around. (16 sts)

Rnd 9: Sc 16.

Rnd 10: *Sc 2, sc2tog; rep from * 3 more times. (12 sts)

Rnd 11: Sc2tog 6 times.

Fasten off yarn and close hole at front of the muzzle.

Glue or sew on 4 mm plastic eyes. Using a single yarn ply from your black yarn or black embroidery thread, apply 1 short st above each eye for an eyebrow.

NOSTRIL (MAKE 2)

In dark brown, ch 3, sl st 3 times in back ridge loop of 3rd ch from hook and fasten off yarn.

Sew nostrils to front of muzzle. Cut (2) 4" pieces of yarn and attach with a fringe knot under the muzzle. Trim short and separate yarn plys with fingers.

BODY

In dark brown, make a 5-st adjustable ring.

Rnd 1: Sc 2 in each st around. (10 sts)

Rnd 2: Sc 2 in each st around. (20 sts)

Rnd 3: *Sc 1, sc 2 in next st; rep from * 9 more times. (30 sts)

Rnd 4: Sc 30.

Rnd 5 : Sc2tog 15 times.

Rnds 6-8: Sc 15.

Rnd 9: *Sc 3, sc2tog; rep from * 2 more times. (12 sts)

MOOSE *(continued)*

Stuff body.

Rnd 10: Sc2tog 6 times. (6 sts)

Fasten off yarn and close hole in the back of the body.

Sew head to the front end of the body.

EAR AND TAIL (MAKE 3)

In dark brown, make a 5-st adjustable ring.

Rnd 1: Sc 2, (sc 1, hdc 1, ch 3, sl st in back ridge loop of 3rd ch from hook, hdc 1, sc 1) in next st, and sc 2. Fasten off yarn.

Attach round end of ears to sides of head. Draw 2 of the leftover yarns tails up through the top of the head, trim short, and separate yarns plys with fingers. For the tail, attach the pointy end of the tail to the back of body.

ANTLER (MAKE 2)

Using tan, loosely ch 8 for a foundation ch.

Rnd 1: Starting in 2nd ch from hook and working in back ridge loops of ch-8; sc 3, ch 3. Starting in 2nd ch from hook and working in back ridge loops of ch-3, sc 2. Cont working in back ridge loops of ch-8; sc 2, ch 3. Starting in 2nd ch from hook and working in back ridge loops of ch-3, sc 2. Cont working in back ridge loops of ch-8; sc 1, sc 3 in back ridge loop of next ch. Turn work so front side of ch-8 is facing up. Starting in front side of the next ch, sc 1, ch 3. Starting in 2nd ch from hook and working in back ridge loops of ch-3, sc 2. Cont working in front side of ch-8; sc 2, ch 3. Starting in 2nd ch from hook and working in back ridge loops of ch-3, sc 2.

Rnd 2: Sc 1 in each st around. Fasten off yarn, leaving a long tail for sewing.

Using the leftover yarn tail and with the RS of the antler piece facing up, sew up the edges of each of the 5 antler prongs using a whip stitch, then close up the base and center seam edges of the antler with a whip stitch. Use the other remaining yarn tail at the base of the ch-8 slip knot to attach antler to head.

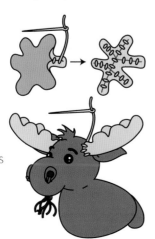

LEG (MAKE 4)

In black, make a 5-st adjustable ring.

Rnd 1: Sc 2 in each st around. (10 sts)

Rnd 2: In bl, sc 10.

Rnd 3: *Sc 3, sc2tog; rep from * 1 more time. (8 sts)

Stuff hoof.

Change to dark brown.

Rnd 4: FPsc 8.

Rnd 5: *Sc 2, sc2tog; rep from * 1 more time. (6 sts)

Rnds 6-8: Sc 6. Fasten off yarn.

Close hole at top of leg. Attach legs to shoulders and hips of body. Tack the insides of the legs to the body to keep legs from splaying out.

Cut green felt into (1) ⅜" by 6½" strip. Bring the scarf around the neck and over the shoulders. Cross the scarf tails, left side over right. Tuck the left tail under the right tail and draw it up and over the top edge of the scarf. Pull gently to tighten the knot and allow the left tail to hang down over the cross point. To keep the tail flat, tack it down with a dab of glue or sew in place if desired. Trim the scarf tails to preferred length and snip 3 small slits into each tail edge to create a fringe.

Attach hanging loop (page 18).

> IF YOU'D LIKE TO ADD A BLACK OR BROWN BEAR TO THIS SET, SIMPLY CHANGE UP THE COLORS FROM THE POLAR BEAR ORNAMENT (PAGE 71).

NATIVITY

wise men,

angels,

and animals gather around a very

special

family

on this

holiest of nights.

CHRISTMAS STAR

······ BEGINNER • FINISHED SIZE: 1¾" TALL/WIDE ······

⫶ MATERIALS ⫶

- Sock weight yarn in dark blue, medium blue, and white
- Hook size C (2.75 mm)
- Polyester fiberfill
- (36) 11/0 seed beads in white or light blue
- (1) 6 mm gold bead for star
- Tapestry needle
- Invisible thread and beading needle
- Scissors
- (1) 10 mm jump ring

Keep sl sts loose to make them easier to work in.

STAR (MAKE 2)

In medium blue, make a 6-st adjustable ring.

Rnd 1: (Sl st 1, ch 2, sl st 1) in each st around.

Rnd 2: *Sl st in next sl st, (sc 1, ch 2, sc 1) in ch-2 sp, sk next sl st, rep from * 5 more times.

Change to dark blue.

Rnd 3: *Sl st in next sl st, sl st in next sc, (sc 1, ch 2, sc 1) in ch-2 sp, sl st in next sc; rep from * 5 more times.

Rnd 4: *Sl st in next 2 sl sts, sl st in next sc, (sc 1, ch 2, sc 1) in ch-2 sp, sl st in next sc, sl st in next sl st; rep from * 5 more times.

Fasten off yarn, leaving a long tail for sewing.

Hold WS of front and back pieces tog, whip stitch around edge of stars, and stuff before closing seams. Draw yarn back and forth through both layers of the star in the center to sink the middle slightly and fasten off yarn.

Using white and the diagram, apply long sts in a star pattern to 1 side of the star. With invisible thread, sew seed beads to the end of each long st. Sew gold bead to center of star.

Attach hanging loop (page 18).

ANGEL

······ INTERMEDIATE • FINISHED SIZE: 3" TALL, 2" WIDE ······

⇌ MATERIALS ⇌

- Sock weight yarn in dark brown, gold, ivory, tan, and white
- Hook size C (2.75 mm)
- Tapestry needle
- Scissors
- Polyester fiberfill
- (8–9) 11/0 seed beads in gold or white
- Invisible thread
- Beading needle
- Craft glue or needle and thread
- (1) 10 mm jump ring

HEAD AND BODY

In tan, make a 6-st adjustable ring.

Rnd 1: Sc 2 in each st around. (12 sts)

Rnd 2: *Sc 2, sc 2 in next st; rep from * 3 more times. (16 sts)

Rnds 3-5: Sc 16.

Rnd 6: *Sc 2, sc2tog; rep from * 3 more times. (12 sts)

Stuff head.

Rnd 7: Sc2tog 6 times.

Change to ivory.

Rnd 8: In bl, *Sc 2, sc 2 in next st; rep from * 1 more time. (8 sts)

Rnd 9: *Sc 3, sc 2 in next st; rep from * 1 more time. (10 sts)

Rnd 10: *Sc 4, sc 2 in next st; rep from * 1 more time. (12 sts)

Rnd 11: Sc 12.

Rnd 12: *Sc 5, sc 2 in next st; rep from * 1 more time. (14 sts)

Rnd 13: *Sc 6, sc 2 in next st; rep from * 1 more time. (16 sts)

Rnd 14: *Sc 3, sc 2 in next st; rep from * 3 more times. (20 sts)

Rnd 15: *Sc 4, sc 2 in next st; rep from *3 more times. (24 sts)

Rnd 16: *Hdc 1, hdc 2 in next st; rep from * 11 more times. (36 sts)

Rnd 17: BPsc 36.

Rnd 18: *Sc 4, sc2tog; rep from * 5 more times. (30 sts)

Stuff body.

Rnd 19: *Sc 1, sc2tog; rep from * 9 more times. (20 sts)

Rnd 20: Sc2tog 10 times. (10 sts)

Fasten off yarn, close hole, and weave in yarn.

COLLAR DETAIL

Rnd 1: With head pointed up and using ivory yarn, (sl st 1, ch 1, sc 1) in one of the exposed fls in rnd 7 (counts as first sc). Cont to work 1 sc in the each of the 5 remaining exposed fls. (6 sts)

Fasten off yarn and weave in ends.

ANGEL *(continued)*

SKIRT DETAIL

Rnd 1: With head pointing down and using ivory yarn, (sl st 1, ch 1, sc 2) in one of the exposed stitches from rnd 17 (counts as 2 sc inc). Cont to work 2 sc in each of the next 35 remaining exposed stitches. (72 sts) Fasten off yarn and weave in ends.

HAND AND ARM (MAKE 2)

Starting with tan, make a 3-st adjustable ring.

Rnd 1: *Sc 2 in each st around. (6 sts)

Rnd 2: Sc 6.

Rnd 3: *Sc 1, sc2tog; rep from * 1 more time. (4 sts)

Change to ivory.

Rnd 4: FPsc 4.

Rnd 5: Sc 2 in each st around. (8 sts)

Rnd 6: In bl, sc 8.

Rnd 7: Sc 8.

Rnd 8: *Sc 2, sc2tog; rep from * 1 more time. (6 sts)

Fasten off yarn and stuff arm lightly. Close hole at top of shoulder.

SLEEVE DETAIL

Rnd 1: With hand pointed up and using ivory yarn, (sl st 1, ch 1, sc 1) in one of the exposed fls in rnd 5. Cont to work 1 sc in each of the 7 remaining exposed fls. (8 sts)

Rnd 2: Sc 8.

Fasten off yarn and weave in ends.

Sew the shoulders to the sides of the body on either side of the neck. Sew the palms of the hands together. Bend the hands up into an upright position and tack in place to the chest of the angel with a few additional sts.

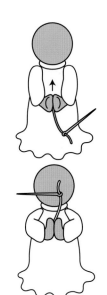

RIGHT WING

In white, make an 8-st adjustable ring.

Row 1: Sc 4, hdc 2 in next 4 sts, turn. (12 sts)

Row 2: Ch 1, (hdc 1, dc 1, ch 3, sl st) in next st, (sc 1, hdc 1, ch 2, sl st) in next st, (sl st 1, sc 1, ch 1, sl st) in next 2 sts, sl st 8, and fasten off yarn.

LEFT WING

In white, make an 8-st adjustable ring.

Rnd 1: Hdc 2 in next 4 sts, sc 4. (12 sts)

Rnd 2: Sl st 8, (sl st 1, ch 1, sc 1, sl st) in next 2 sts, (sl st 1, ch 2, hdc 1, sc 1) in next st, (sl st 1, ch 3, dc 1, hdc 1) in next st, sl st, and fasten off yarn.

Place round sides of wings at the center of the back and sew in place.

HAIR

In dark brown, make an 8-st adjustable ring.

Rnd 1: Sc 2 in each st around. (16 sts)

Rnd 2: *Sc 3, sc 2 in next st; rep from * 3 more times. (20 sts)

Rnd 3: (Sl st 1, hdc 2) in next st; (hdc 1, sc 1) in next st; sl st 1, (sc 1, hdc 1) in next st, (hdc 2, st st 1) in next st, sk 1, sl st 1, sk 1, sl st 1, hdc 2 in next 7 sts, sl st 1, sk 1, sl st 1, sk 1. (29 sts)

Rnd 4: Sl st 1, sc 4 , sl st 1, sc 4, sl st 1, sk 2, sl st 1, hdc 2 in next st, hdc 10, hdc 2 in next st, sl st 1, sk 2, and fasten off yarn in next st. (27 sts)

Fasten off yarn, leaving a long tail for sewing.

Place hair on head and sew edge of hair to the temples and front of the forehead. Leave the back of the hair loose.

HALO

In gold, ch 15. Sl st in first ch to form a ring.

Sew the halo to the back of the hair, leaving the upper half of the halo loose.

Add gold seed beads to halo and white seed beads to wings using invisible thread and a beading needle.

Attach hanging loop (page 18).

BABY IN THE MANGER

······ INTERMEDIATE • FINISHED SIZE: 2¼" TALL, 1¼" WIDE ······

⇌ MATERIALS ⇌

- Sock weight yarn in dark brown, ivory, light yellow, medium yellow, and tan
- Hook size C (2.75 mm)
- Tapestry needle
- Scissors
- Polyester fiberfill
- (1) 10 mm jump ring

MANGER

With dark brown, make an 8-st adjustable ring.

Rnd 1: Sc 2 in each st around. (16 sts)

Rnd 2: *Sc 3, sc 2 in next st; rep from * 3 more times. (20 sts)

Rnd 3: BPsc 20.

Rnds 4-12: Sc 20.

Rnd 13: BPsc 20.

Rnd 14: *Sc 3, sc2tog; rep from * 3 more times. (16 sts)

Rnd 15: Sc2tog 8 times. (8 sts)

Fasten off yarn and close hole. Flatten manger the long way and tack down shaping with a few sts in dark brown.

HEAD AND BODY

In tan, make a 4-st adjustable ring.

Rnd 1: Sc 2 in each st around. (8 sts)

Rnd 2: *Sc 1, sc 2 in next st; rep from * 3 more times. (12 sts)

Rnds 3-4: Sc 12.

Rnd 5: *Sc 1, sc2tog; rep from * 3 more times. (8 sts)

Stuff head.

Rnd 6: *Sc 2, sc2tog; rep from * 1 more time. (6 sts)

Change to ivory.

Rnd 7: In bl, *sc 2, sc 2 in next st; rep from * 1 more time. (8 sts)

Rnd 8: *Sc 3, sc 2 in next st; rep from * 1 more time. (10 sts)

Rnd 9: *Sc 4, sc 2 in next st; rep from * 1 more time. (12 sts)

Rnd 10: Sc 12.

Rnd 11: *Sc 4, sc2tog; rep from * 1 more time. (10 sts)

Rnd 12: Sc 10.

Rnd 13: *Sc 3, sc2tog; rep from * 1 more time. (8 sts)

Stuff body.

Rnd 14: *Sc 2, sc2tog; rep from * 1 more time. (6 sts)

Fasten off yarn, close hole, and weave in yarn.

BABY IN THE MANGER *(continued)*

COLLAR DETAIL

Rnd 1: With head pointed up and using ivory yarn, (sl st 1, ch 1, sc 1) in 1 of the exposed fls in rnd 6. Cont to work 1 sc in each of the 5 remaining exposed fls. (6 sts)

Fasten off yarn and weave in ends.

ARM (MAKE 2)

In tan, make a 4-st adjustable ring.

Rnd 1: Sc 4.

Change to ivory.

Rnds 2-4: Sc 4.

Fasten off yarn and close hole.

Attach arms at the sides of the body under the collar.

HEAD COVER

In ivory, make a 6-st adjustable ring.

Rnd 1: *Sc 1, sc 2 in next st; rep from * 2 more times. (9 sts)

Rnd 2: *Sc 2, sc 2 in next st; rep from * 2 more times. (12 sts)

Rnd 3: *Sc 3, sc 2 in next st; rep from * 2 more times. (15 sts)

Rnd 4: Sc 15.

Fasten off yarn. Place cover over back of head and sew in place. Sew bottom edge of head cover to back of body below the neck.

Cut out (8) 4" pieces of light yellow and (8) 4" pieces of medium yellow yarn. Mix up and apply the yarn to the inside of the manger using fringe knots. Separate the yarn plys with a tapestry needle or your fingers.

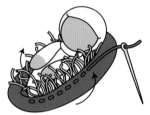

Gently curl the manger around the lower half and the body. Using dark brown, attach the bottom and sides of the manger to the back of the body and head.

Trim the hay in the manger.

MANGER LEG (MAKE 4)

With dark brown, make a 6-st adjustable ring.

Rnd 1: Sc 6.

Fasten off yarn.

Attach open edges of legs to the bottom of the manger.

Attach hanging loop (page 18).

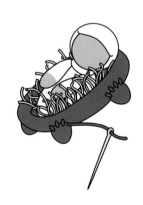

MARY

······ INTERMEDIATE • FINISHED SIZE: 3" TALL, 2" WIDE ······

⇌ MATERIALS ⇌

- Sock weight yarn in dark brown, light blue, medium blue, and tan
- Hook size C (2.75 mm)
- Tapestry needle
- Scissors
- Polyester fiberfill
- (1) 10 mm jump ring

HEAD AND BODY

In tan, make a 6-st adjustable ring.

Rnd 1: Sc 2 in each st around. (12 sts)

Rnd 2: *Sc 2, sc 2 in next st; rep from * 3 more times. (16 sts)

Rnds 3-5: Sc 16.

Rnd 6: *Sc 2, sc2tog; rep from * 3 more times. (12 sts)

Stuff head.

Rnd 7: Sc2tog 6 times.

Change to light blue.

Rnd 8: In bl, *sc 2, sc 2 in next st; rep from * 1 more time. (8 sts)

Rnd 9: *Sc 3, sc 2 in next st; rep from * 1 more time. (10 sts)

Rnd 10: *Sc 4, sc 2 in next st; rep from * 1 more time. (12 sts)

Rnds 11-12: Sc 12.

Rnd 13: *Sc 5, sc 2 in next st; rep from * 1 more time. (14 sts)

Rnd 14: Sc 14.

Rnd 15: *Sc 6, sc 2 in next st; rep from * 1 more time. (16 sts)

Rnds 16-17: Sc 16.

Rnd 18: BPsc 16.

Stuff body.

Rnd 19: Sc2tog 8 times.

Fasten off yarn, close hole, and weave in yarn.

COLLAR DETAIL

Rnd 1: With head pointed up and using light blue yarn, (sl st 1, ch 1, sc 1) in one of the exposed fls in rnd 7 (counts as first sc). Cont to work 1 sc in each of the 5 remaining exposed fls. (6 sts)

Fasten off yarn and weave in ends.

SKIRT DETAIL

Rnd 1: With head pointing down and using light blue yarn, (sl st 1, ch 1, sc 1) in one of the exposed stitches from rnd 18. Sc 2 in next st, then rep the pattern [sc 1, sc 2 in next st] in the 14 remaining exposed stitches of rnd 18. (24 sts)

Fasten off yarn and weave in ends.

MARY *(continued)*

HAND AND ARM (MAKE 2)

Starting with tan, make a 3-st adjustable ring.

Rnd 1: * Sc 2 in each st around. (6 sts)

Rnd 2: Sc 6.

Rnd 3: *Sc 1, sc2tog; rep from * 1 more time. (4 sts)

Change to light blue.

Rnd 4: FPsc 4.

Rnd 5: Sc 2 in each st around. (8 sts)

Rnd 6: In bl, sc 8.

Rnd 7: Sc 8.

Rnd 8: *Sc 2, sc2tog; rep from * 1 more time. (6 sts)

Fasten off yarn and stuff arm lightly. Close hole at top of shoulder.

SLEEVE DETAIL

Rnd 1: With hand pointed up and using light blue yarn, (sl st 1, ch 1, sc 1) in 1 of the exposed fls in rnd 5. Cont to work 1 sc in each of the 7 remaining exposed fls. (8 sts)

Rnd 2: Sc 8.

Fasten off yarn and weave in ends.

Sew the shoulders to the sides of the body on either side of the neck. Sew the palms of the hands together. Bend the hands up into an upright position and tack in place to the chest of the body with a few additional sts.

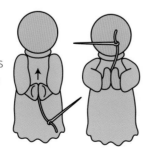

HAIR COVER

In medium blue, make an 8-st adjustable ring.

Rnd 1: Sc 2 in each st around. (16 sts)

Rnd 2: *Sc 3, sc 2 in next st; rep from * 3 more times. (20 sts)

Row 3: Sc 14, turn. (14 sts)

Rows 4-10: Ch 1, sc 14, turn. (16 sts)

Rnd 11: Ch 1, sc 14, sl st 8 along edge of rows 10 to 3, BPsc 6, sl st 8 along the edge of rows 3 to 10, and fasten off yarn.

Place hair cover on head and tack in place with a few sts along the front and sides of the face, and the tops of the shoulders. You can also apply a few sts between the back of the head and cover to keep it closer to the head in the back if you desire.

With dark brown yarn, apply a grouping of 3 long sts from the top of the forehead to the left side of the head (working just under the edge of the hair cover). Allow sts to hang loosely and repeat the process, working to the right side of the head.

Attach hanging loop (page 18).

TO MAKE THE NATIVITY LARGER AS A PLAYSET FOR CHILDREN, USE WORSTED WEIGHT YARN AND A SIZE F (3.75 MM) HOOK.

JOSEPH

······ INTERMEDIATE • FINISHED SIZE: 3" TALL, 2" WIDE ······

⇌ MATERIALS ⇌

- Sock weight yarn in blue, burgundy, dark brown, and tan
- Hook size C (2.75 mm)
- Tapestry needle
- Scissors
- Polyester Fiberfill
- Ivory felt
- (1) 10 mm jump ring

HEAD AND BODY

In tan, make a 6-st adjustable ring.

Rnd 1: Sc 2 in each st around. (12 sts)

Rnd 2: *Sc 2, sc 2 in next st; rep from * 3 more times. (16 sts)

Rnds 3-5: Sc 16.

Rnd 6: *Sc 2, sc2tog; rep from * 3 more times. (12 sts)

Stuff head.

Rnd 7: Sc2tog 6 times. (6 sts)

Change to burgundy.

Rnd 8: In bl, *sc 2, sc 2 in next st; rep from * 1 more time. (8 sts)

Rnd 9: *Sc 3, sc 2 in next st; rep from * 1 more time. (10 sts)

Rnd 10: *Sc 4, sc 2 in next st; rep from * 1 more time. (12 sts)

Rnds 11-12: Sc 12.

Rnd 13: *Sc 5, sc 2 in next st; rep from * 1 more time. (14 sts)

Rnd 14: Sc 14.

Rnd 15: *Sc 6, sc 2 in next st; rep from * 1 more time. (16 sts)

Rnd 16: Sc 16.

Rnd 17: *Sc 7, sc 2 in next st; rep from * 1 more time. (18 sts)

Rnd 18: BPsc 18.

Stuff body.

Rnd 19: *Sc 1, sc2tog; rep from * 5 more times. (12 sts)

Rnd 20: Sc2tog 6 times. (6 sts)

Fasten off yarn, close hole, and weave in yarn.

COLLAR DETAIL

Rnd 1: With head pointed up and using burgundy yarn, (sl st 1, ch 1, sc 1) in one of the exposed fls in rnd 7 (counts as first sc). Cont to work 1 sc in the each of the 5 remaining exposed fls.

Fasten off yarn and weave in ends.

JOSEPH *(continued)*

ROBE DETAIL

Rnd 1: With head pointing down and using burgundy yarn, (sl st 1, ch 1, sc 1) in one of the exposed stitches from rnd 18. Sc 2 in next st, then rep the pattern [sc 1, sc 2 in next st] in the 16 remaining exposed stitches of rnd 18. (27 sts)

Fasten off yarn and weave in ends.

BELT

With dark brown yarn, ch 26. Wrap ch around waist of body and tie in a square knot in front. Trim yarn tails fairly short and separate yarn plys with tapestry needle or fingers.

HAND AND ARM (MAKE 2)

Starting with tan, make a 3-st adjustable ring.

Rnd 1: * Sc 2 in each st around. (6 sts)

Rnd 2: Sc 6.

Rnd 3: *Sc 1, sc2tog; rep from * 1 more time. (4 sts)

Change to burgundy.

Rnd 4: FPsc 4.

Rnd 5: Sc 2 in each st around. (8 sts)

Rnd 6: In bl, sc 8.

Rnd 7: Sc 8.

Rnd 8: *Sc 2, sc2tog; rep from * 1 more time. (6 sts)

Fasten off yarn and stuff arm lightly. Close hole at top of shoulder.

SLEEVE DETAIL

Rnd 1: With hand pointed up and using burgundy yarn, (sl st 1, ch 1, sc 1) in one of the exposed fls in rnd 5. Cont to work 1 sc in each of the 7 remaining exposed fls. (8 sts)

Rnd 2: Sc 8.

Fasten off yarn and weave in ends.

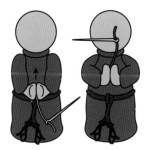

Sew the shoulders to the sides of the body on either side of the neck. Sew the palms of the hands together. Bend the hands up into an upright position and tack in place to the chest of the body with a few additional sts.

HEAD COVER

In blue, make an 8-st adjustable ring.

Rnd 1: Sc 2 in each st around. (16 sts)

Rnd 2: *Sc 3, sc 2 in next st; rep from * 3 more times. (20 sts)

Row 3: Sc 14, turn. (14 sts)

Rows 4-10: Ch 1, sc 14, turn. (14 sts)

Rnd 11: Ch 1, sc 14, sl st 8 along edge of rows 10 to 3, BPsc 6, sl st 8 along the edge of rows 3 to 10, and fasten off yarn.

Place head cover on head and tack in place with a few sts along the front and sides of the face, and the tops of the shoulders. You can also apply a few sts between the back of the head and cover to keep it closer to the head in the back if you desire.

With dark brown yarn, cut (8) 4" pieces and attach them to the bottom of the face with fringe knots. Trim relatively short and separate yarn ply with tapestry needle or fingers. Trim a second time to shape the beard if needed.

With dark brown yarn, apply 3 droopy long sts directly above the fringe knots of the beard to the side of the cheek for half a mustache. Repeat on other cheek for 2nd half of mustache.

HEAD BAND

With dark brown yarn, ch 16. Wrap ch around top of head over hair cover and secure in back. Tack down ch with a few brown sts to hold it in place if needed.

Attach hanging loop (page 18).

SHEPHERD AND KINGS

······ INTERMEDIATE • FINISHED SIZE: 3" TALL, 2" WIDE ······

⇆ MATERIALS ⇆

- Sock weight yarn in:
  - Skin colors: dark brown and tan
  - Robe colors: brown, gold, green, purple, and red
  - Head cover colors: dark brown, gold, green, ivory, purple, and red
  - Hair colors: black, charcoal, and ivory
- Hook size C (2.75 mm)
- Tapestry needle
- (4½") 16-gauge copper or bronze wire; round-nose and flat pliers
- (3) Assorted ½"–¾" fancy gold beads
- (3) 11/0 gold seed beads
- (3) ¼" gold beads
- (1) 4 mm white bead
- (1) 6 mm gold bead
- Ivory felt
- Scissors
- Polyester fiberfill
- Invisible thread and beading needle
- (4) 10 mm jump rings

HEAD AND BODY

In skin color, make a 6-st adjustable ring.

Rnd 1: Sc 2 in each st around. (12 sts)

Rnd 2: *Sc 2, sc 2 in next st; rep from * 3 more times. (16 sts)

Rnds 3-5: Sc 16.

Rnd 6: *Sc 2, sc2tog; rep from * 3 more times. (12 sts)

Stuff head.

Rnd 7: Sc2tog 6 times. (6 sts)

Change to robe color.

Rnd 8: In bl, *sc 2, sc 2 in next st; rep from * 1 more time. (8 sts)

Rnd 9: *Sc 3, sc 2 in next st; rep from * 1 more time. (10 sts)

Rnd 10: *Sc 4, sc 2 in next st; rep from * 1 more time. (12 sts)

Rnds 11-12: Sc 12.

Rnd 13: *Sc 5, sc 2 in next st; rep from * 1 more time. (14 sts)

Rnd 14: Sc 14.

Rnd 15: *Sc 6, sc 2 in next st; rep from * 1 more time. (16 sts)

Rnd 16: Sc 16.

For kings only: change to gold.

Rnd 17: *Sc 7, sc 2 in next st; rep from * 1 more time. (18 sts)

Rnd 18: BPsc 18.

Stuff body. For kings only: change to robe color.

Rnd 19: *Sc 1, sc2tog; rep from * 5 more times. (12 sts)

Rnd 20: Sc2tog 6 times. (6 sts)

Fasten off yarn, close hole, and weave in yarn.

COLLAR DETAIL

Rnd 1: With head pointed up and using gold for kings and dark brown for shepherds, (sl st 1, ch 1, sc 1) in one of the exposed fls in rnd 7 (counts as first sc). Cont to work 1 sc in the each of the next 4 exposed fls, leaving one st unworked to create a space at the front of the collar. (5 sts)

Fasten off yarn and weave in ends.

SHEPHERD AND KINGS *(continued)*

ROBE DETAIL

Rnd 1: With head pointing down and using gold yarn for kings and dark brown for shepherds, (sl st 1, ch 1, sc 1) in one of the exposed stitches from rnd 18. Sc 2 in next st, then rep the pattern [sc 1, sc 2 in next st] in the 16 remaining exposed stitches of rnd 18. (27 sts)

Fasten off yarn and weave in ends.

ROBE PANEL

With ivory felt, cut (1) ½" by 1¾" rectangle. Taper the rectangle by trimming down the long sides at an angle so one end of the rectangle is ½" and the opposite end is ¼". Line up the small end of the rectangle with the space at the collar under the head. Glue or sew the robe panel down the front of the body and trim bottom edge if needed. With gold for kings and brown for shepherd, embroider a chain stitch along the sides of the robe panel.

BELT

With tan for shepherd or gold for kings, ch 26. Wrap ch around waist of body and tie in a square knot in front. For kings, slide knot over just to the left or right of the front robe panel. Trim yarn tails fairly short and separate yarn plys with tapestry needle or fingers.

HAND AND ARM (MAKE 2)

Starting with skin color, make a 3-st adjustable ring.

Rnd 1: *Sc 2 in each st around. (6 sts)

Rnd 2: Sc 6.

Rnd 3: *Sc 1, sc2tog; rep from * 1 more time. (4 sts)

Change to robe color.

Rnd 4: FPsc 4.

Rnd 5: Sc 2 in each st around. (8 sts)

Rnd 6: In bl, sc 8.

Rnd 7: Sc 8.

Rnd 8: *Sc 2, sc2tog; rep from * 1 more time. (6 sts)

Fasten off yarn and stuff arm lightly. Close hole at top of shoulder.

SLEEVE DETAIL

Rnd 1: With hand pointed up and using robe color yarn, (sl st 1, ch 1, sc 1) in one of the exposed fls in rnd 5. Cont to work 1 sc in each of the 7 remaining exposed fls. (8 sts)

For kings only, change to gold.

Rnd 2: Sc 8.

Fasten off yarn and weave in ends.

Sew the shoulders to the sides of the body on either side of the neck. For kings, sew the tips of the hands together.

KING'S GIFTS

Cut a long length of invisible thread, fold it in half to double it up, and thread the ends onto a beading needle. Thread the needle through a gold seed bead and through the loop at the end of the folded thread to secure the bead. Thread the needle through (1) ¼" gold bead and (1) ½" to ¾" fancy gold bead to create a stack of beads.

Sew the bead stack to the palms of the connected hands and fasten off yarn. If needed, use robe color and draw the arms closer to the body with a few sts between the arms and the sides of the chest and fasten off yarn. You can also apply a few drops of glue between the back of the bead stack and the arms to keep everything in place.

KING CROWN #1

In robe color, make an 8-st adjustable ring.

Rnd 1: Sc 2 in each st around. (16 sts)

Rnd 2: *Sc 1, sc 2 in next st; rep from * 7 more times. (24 sts)

Rnd 3: Sc 24.

Rnd 4: *Sc 2, sc2tog; rep from * 5 more times. (18 sts)

Change to gold.

Rnd 5: *Sc 7, sc2tog; rep from * 1 more time. (16 sts)

Rnd 6: FPsc 16.

Fasten off yarn.

Lightly stuff crown. Push head into crown (it will be a snug fit) and sew gold hat brim to head. In gold, draw 2 long sts over the top of the hat from front to back (1 right of center and 1 left of center) and pull tightly to shape hat. Fasten off yarn.

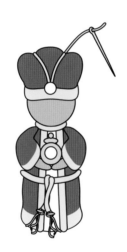

If desired, use invisible thread and a beading needle and add a small 4 mm white bead to the front of the crown for a pearl detail.

KING CROWN #2

In robe color, make a 6-st adjustable ring.

Rnd 1: Sc 2 in each st around. (12 sts)

Rnd 2: *Sc 1, sc 2 in next st; rep from * 7 more times. (18 sts)

Rnds 3-4: Sc 18.

Change to gold.

Rnd 5: Sc 18.

Rnd 6: *Sc 2, sc 2 in next st; rep from * 7 more times. (24 sts)

Rnd 7: Hdc 24.

Rnd 8: *Sc 2, sc2tog; rep from * 7 more times. (18 sts)

Fasten off yarn.

Roll the gold brim of hat up until rnd 8 lines up with rnd 5. With gold yarn, sew rnd 8 to rnd 5 with a running st.

With robe color, wind long sts around the rolled-up gold brim, pulling firmly to crimp the brim shape.

If desired, use invisible thread and a beading needle and add a small 6 mm gold bead to the top of the crown.

KING CROWN #3

In robe color, make a 3-st adjustable ring.

Rnd 1: Sc 2 in each st around. (6 sts)

Rnd 2: *Sc 1, sc 2 in next st; rep from * 2 more times. (9 sts)

Rnd 3: *Sc 2, sc 2 in next st; rep from * 2 more times. (12 sts)

Rnd 4: *Sc 3, sc 2 in next st; rep from * 2 more times. (15 sts)

Rnd 5: *Sc 4, sc 2 in next st; rep from * 2 more times. (18 sts)

Rnd 6: Sc 18.

Change to gold.

Rnd 7: FPsc 18.

Row 8: BPsc 6, turn. (6 sts)

Row 9: Ch 1, sc 2 in next st, sc 4, sc 2 in next st, turn. (8 sts)

Rnd 10: Ch 1, sc 8, sl st 2 along edge of rows 9 to 8, BPsc 12, sl st 2 along edge of rows 8 to 9, and fasten off yarn.

Push head into crown (it will be a snug fit) and sew gold hat brim to head.

If desired, use invisible thread and a beading needle and add a row of gold seed beads to the front half of the brim.

SHEPHERD AND KINGS (continued)

SHEPHERD HEAD COVER

In ivory, make an 8-st adjustable ring.

Rnd 1: Sc 2 in each st around. (16 sts)

Rnd 2: *Sc 3, sc 2 in next st; rep from * 3 more times. (20 sts)

Row 3: Sc 14, turn. (14 sts)

Rows 4-10: Ch 1, sc 14, turn. (16 sts)

Rnd 11: Ch 1, sc 14, sl st 8 along edge of rows 10 to 3, BPsc 6, sl st 8 along the edge of rows 3 to 10, and fasten off yarn.

Place head cover on head and tack in place with a few sts along the front and sides of the face, and the tops of the shoulders. You can also apply a few sts between the back of the head and cover to keep it closer to the head in the back if you desire.

SHEPHERD HEADBAND

With dark brown yarn, ch 16. Wrap ch around top of head over hair cover and secure in back. Tack down ch with a few sts to hold it in place if needed.

CROOK

Using wire cutters and 16-gauge brass or bronze wire, cut (1) 4½" piece and straighten it. Using round nose pliers, curl a small circle at the end of the wire, then curl over the last 1" of the wire for the bent end of the crook. Follow template for reference.

Insert the crook through the hands of the shepherd. Using dark brown yarn, pose the arms and tack them to the body to hold them in place. Apply some craft glue to the underside of the hands where the crook exits the hand to keep the crook in place.

BEARD AND MUSTACHE

Using ivory, black, or dark grey yarn, cut (8 to 15) 4" to 5" pieces of yarn and attach to the front of the face for a beard. For a mustache, apply 3 droopy long sts directly above the fringe knots from the center of the face to the side of the cheek for half a mustache. Repeat on other cheek for 2nd half of mustache.

Attach hanging loop (page 18).

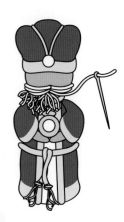

CAMEL

······ INTERMEDIATE • FINISHED SIZE: 3" TALL, 2½" LONG, 1½" WIDE ······

⇟ MATERIALS ⇟

- Sock weight yarn in black, dark brown, and tan
- Hook size C (2.75 mm)
- Tapestry needle
- Scissors
- Yellow felt
- Green felt
- Gold felt
- (8) Silver 6/0 "E" beads
- Polyester fiberfill
- (2) 4 mm plastic eyes
- (1) 10 mm jump ring

HEAD AND MUZZLE

In tan, make a 6-st adjustable ring.

Rnd 1: Sc 2 in each st around. (12 sts)

Rnd 2: *Sc 2, sc 2 in next st; rep from * 3 more times. (16 sts)

Rnds 3-5: Sc 16.

Rnd 6: *Sc 2, sc2tog; rep from * 3 more times. (12 sts)

Stuff head.

Rnd 7: *Sc 1, sc2tog; rep from * 3 more times. (8 sts)

Rnd 8: *Sc 1, sc 2 in next st; rep from * 3 more times. (12 sts)

Rnd 9: *Sc 2, sc 2 in next st; rep from * 3 more times. (16 sts)

Rnd 10: *Sc 2, sc2tog; rep from * 3 more times. (12 sts)

Stuff muzzle.

Rnd 11: Sc2tog 6 times.

Fasten off yarn and close hole at front of the muzzle.

Glue or sew on 4 mm plastic eyes. Using a single yarn ply from your black yarn or black embroidery thread, apply 1 short st above each eye for an eyebrow.

With black yarn, apply a long st to each side of the muzzle for a nostril.

EAR (MAKE 2)

In tan, make a 5-st adjustable ring.

Rnd 1: Sc 2, (sc 1, ch 2, sl st in back ridge loop of 2nd ch from hook, sc 1) in next st, sc 2.

Attach flat end of ears to sides of head. Draw 2 of the leftover yarns tails up through the top of the head, trim short, and separate yarns plys with fingers for a bit of hair.

BODY

*For the hump of the camel, please note that the sts are offset in rnds 5 to 8 to account for the twisting that occurs when working in a spiral.

In tan, make a 5-st adjustable ring.

Rnd 1: Sc 2 in each st around. (10 sts)

Rnd 2: *Sc 1, sc 2 in next st; rep from * 4 more times. (15 sts)

CAMEL *(continued)*

Rnd 3: (Neck opening) Sc 5, ch 5, sk 5, sc 5. (15 sts)

Rnd 4: Sc 5, sc in each st of ch-5, sc 5. (15 sts)

Rnd 5: Sc 5, hdc 2 in next 5 sts, sc 5. (20 sts)

Rnd 6: Sc 10, sc 2 in next 4 sts, sc 6. (24 sts)

Rnd 7: Sc 8, sc2tog 6 times, sc 4. (18 sts)

Rnd 8: *Sc 1, sc2tog; rep from * 5 more times. (12 sts)

Rnd 9: Sc2tog 6 times. (6 sts)

Fasten off yarn and close hole.

NECK

Rnd 1: In tan, (sl st, ch 1, sc 1) in one of the neck opening sts (counts as first sc). Cont to work 1 sc in each of the remaining 9 sts around the inside of the neck opening. (10 sts)

Rnds 2-4: Sc 10.

Fasten off yarn, leaving a long tail. Stuff body.

Attach bottom of head to open neck edge. Use leftover yarn tails to close any holes that may appear in the corners in rnd 1 of the neck.

TAIL

In tan, loosely ch 5.

Starting in 2nd ch from hook and working in back ridge loops, sl st 4 and fasten off yarn.

Attach tapered end of tail to back of body.

LEG (MAKE 4)

In tan, make a 5-st adjustable ring.

Rnd 1: Sc 2 in each st around. (10 sts)

Rnd 2: Sc 10.

Rnd 3: *Sc 3, sc2tog; rep from * 1 more times. (8 sts)

Stuff foot.

Rnd 4: Sc 8.

Rnd 5: *Sc 2, sc2tog; rep from * 1 more time. (6 sts)

Rnds 6-8: Sc 6. Fasten off yarn.

Close hole at top of leg.

Attach legs to shoulders and hips of body. Tack the insides of the legs to the body to keep legs from splaying out. With black yarn, loop a long st over the front of the foot to define the toes, pulling tightly before fastening off.

BEADED BRIDLE

In dark brown, wrap the yarn around the muzzle twice and secure. Draw a 10" to 12" piece of dark brown yarn out through the wrapped yarn around where the corner of the camel's mouth would be. Using (8) beads, string 1 onto the yarn every ¼". Thread the needle through the bead a 2nd time to hold its place on the yarn before adding the next bead. Secure the end of the yarn to the other side of muzzle wrap and fasten off yarn.

SADDLE

Cut (1) 2" by ¾" rectangle of green colored felt, (1) 1½" by ⅝" rectangle of yellow felt, and (1) ⅝" circle of gold felt.

Center and glue or sew down the yellow felt to the green felt. Fringe the short edges of the green edges with about 5 slits each. Glue or sew the completed saddle over the hump and sides of the camel. Glue or sew the gold felt circle to the top of the saddle.

Attach hanging loop to the bottom of the back of the neck (page 18).

DONKEY

······ INTERMEDIATE • FINISHED SIZE: 3" TALL, 2½" LONG, 1½" WIDE ······

⇌ MATERIALS ⇌

- Sock weight yarn in black, light grey, and ivory
- Hook size C (2.75 mm)
- Tapestry needle
- Violet felt
- Brown felt
- Scissors
- Polyester fiberfill
- (2) 4 mm plastic eyes
- (1) 10 mm jump ring

HEAD AND MUZZLE

In light grey, make a 6-st adjustable ring.

Rnd 1: Sc 2 in each st around. (12 sts)

Rnd 2: *Sc 2, sc 2 in next st; rep from * 3 more times. (16 sts)

Rnds 3-5: Sc 16.

Rnd 6: *Sc 2, sc2tog; rep from * 3 more times. (12 sts)

Stuff head.

Rnd 7: *Sc 1, sc2tog; rep from * 3 more times. (8 sts)

Rnd 8: Sc 2 in each st around. (16 sts)

Change to ivory.

Rnd 9: Sc 16.

Rnd 10: *Sc 2, sc2tog; rep from * 3 more times. (12 sts)

Stuff muzzle.

Rnd 11: Sc2tog 6 times.

Fasten off yarn and close hole at front of the muzzle.

Glue or sew on 4 mm plastic eyes. Using a single yarn ply from your black yarn or black embroidery thread, apply 1 short st above each eye for an eyebrow.

NOSTRIL (MAKE 2)

In ivory, ch 3, sl st 3 times in back ridge loop of 3rd ch from hook. Fasten off yarn.

Sew nostrils to front of muzzle.

EAR (MAKE 2)

In light grey, loosely ch 8.

Rnd 1: Starting in 2nd ch from hook and working in back ridge loops, sl st 2, sc 3, hdc 1, (hdc 1, ch 2, sl st in back ridge loop of 2nd ch from hook, hdc 1) in back ridge loop of next st. Rotate ch so front side of ch is facing up. Starting in front side of the next ch, hdc 1, sc 3, sl st 1 in front side of next ch, and fasten off yarn.

Weave yarn tails in at larger end of ear. Attach smaller end of ears to top of head.

DONKEY *(continued)*

BODY

In tan, make a 5-st adjustable ring.

Rnd 1: Sc 2 in each st around. (10 sts)

Rnd 2: *Sc 1, sc 2 in next st; rep from * 4 more times. (15 sts)

Rnd 3: (Neck opening) Sc 5, ch 5, sk 5, sc 5. (15 sts)

Rnd 4: Sc 5, sc in each st of ch-5, sc 5. (15 sts)

Rnds 5-7: Sc 15.

Rnd 8: *Sc 3, sc2tog; rep from * 2 more times. (12 sts)

Rnd 9: Sc2tog 6 times. (6 sts)

Fasten off yarn and close hole.

NECK

Rnd 1: In light grey, (sl st, ch 1, sc 1) in one of the neck opening sts (counts as first sc). Cont to work 1 sc in each of the remaining 9 sts around the inside of the neck opening. (10 sts)

Rnds 2-3: Sc 10.

Fasten off yarn, leaving a long tail. Stuff body.

Attach bottom of head to open neck edge. Use leftover yarn tails to close any holes that may appear in the corners in rnd 1 of the neck.

Cut (8 to 10) 4" pieces of black yarn and attach them using a fringe knot starting between the ears and down the back of the head in a straight line. Trim to about ½" and separate yarn plys using a tapestry needle or your fingers. Do a final trim to shape the mane.

TAIL

In light grey, loosely ch 7.

Starting in 2nd ch from hook and working in back ridge loops, sl st 6 and fasten off yarn.

Cut (2) 5" pieces of black yarn. Hold yarn strands together and apply them to the end of the tail using a fringe knot. Trim short and separate yarn plys using a tapestry needle or your fingers.

Attach tail using leftover yarn tails to back of body.

LEG (MAKE 4)

In black, make a 5-st adjustable ring.

Rnd 1: Sc 2 in each st around. (10 sts)

Rnd 2: In bl, sc 10.

Rnd 3: *Sc 3, sc2tog; rep from * 1 more time. (8 sts)

Stuff hoof.

Change to light grey.

Rnd 4: FPsc 8.

Rnd 5: *Sc 2, sc2tog; rep from * 1 more time. (6 sts)

Rnds 6-8: Sc 6. Fasten off yarn.

Close hole at top of leg. Attach legs to shoulders and hips of body. Tack the insides of the legs to the body to keep legs from splaying out.

SADDLE

Cut (1) 1" by 1¾" rectangle of violet felt and (1) ¾" by 1¼" rectangle of brown felt.

Center and glue or sew the brown felt to the violet felt. Fringe the short edges of the violet felt with about 7 slits each. Glue or sew the completed saddle over the back of the donkey.

Attach hanging loop to the back of the head (page 18).

RESOURCES

ABBREVIATIONS

* Repeat instructions following the asterisk[s] as directed

approx	approximately
beg	begin(ning)
bl	back loop(s)
BPsc	back post single crochet
CC	contrasting color
ch(s)	chain(s) or chain stitch(es)
ch-	refers to chain, or chain space previously made, such as "ch-1 space"
cont	continue(ing)(s)
dc	double crochet(s)
dec(s)	decrease(ing)(s)
fl	front loop(s)
FPsc	front post single crochet
hdc	half double crochet(s)
hdc2tog	half double crochet 2 stitches together—1 stitch decreased
inc(s)	increase(ing)(s)
lp(s)	loop(s)
MC	main color
mm	millimeter
pm	place marker
rep(s)	repeat(s)
rnd(s)	round(s)
RS	right side
sc	single crochet(s)
sc2tog	single crochet 2 stitches together—1 stitch decreased
sk	skip
sl	slip
sl st(s)	slip stitch(es)
sp(s)	space(s)
st(s)	stitch(es)
tog	together
tr	treble crochet
WS	wrong side
YO(s)	yarn over(s)
yd(s)	yard(s)

PROJECT RANKING

Beginner: Projects for first-time crocheters using basic stitches; minimal shaping.

Easy: Projects using yarn with basic stitches, repetitive stitch patterns, simple color changes, and simple shaping and finishing.

Intermediate: Projects using a variety of techniques, such as basic lace patterns or color patterns; midlevel shaping and finishing.

Experienced: Projects with intricate stitch patterns, techniques, and dimension, such as non-repeating patterns, multicolor techniques, fine threads, small hooks, detailed shaping, and refined finishing.

CROCHET HOOK SIZES

Millimeter	U.S. Size*
2.25 mm	B-1
2.75 mm	C-2
3.25 mm	D-3
3.5 mm	E-4
3.75 mm	F-5
4 mm	G-6
4.5 mm	7
5 mm	H-8
5.5 mm	I-9
6 mm	J-10
6.5 mm	K-10½
8 mm	L-11
9 mm	M/N-13

*Letter or number may vary. Rely on the millimeter sizing.

STANDARD YARN WEIGHTS

YARN-WEIGHT SYMBOL AND CATEGORY NAME	SUPER FINE	FINE	LIGHT	MEDIUM	BULKY	SUPER BULKY
TYPES OF YARN IN CATEGORY	Sock, Fingering, Baby	Sport, Baby	DK, Light Worsted	Worsted, Afghan, Aran	Chunky, Craft, Rug	Bulky, Roving
CROCHET GAUGE* RANGE IN SINGLE CROCHET TO 4"	21 to 32 sts	16 to 20 sts	12 to 17 sts	11 to 14 sts	8 to 11 sts	5 to 9 sts
RECOMMENDED HOOK IN METRIC SIZE RANGE	2.25 to 3.5 mm	3.5 to 4.5 mm	4.5 to 5.5 mm	5.5 to 6.5 mm	6.5 to 9 mm	9 mm and larger
RECOMMENDED HOOK IN U.S. SIZE RANGE	B-1 to E-4	E-4 to 7	7 to I-9	I-9 to K-10½	K-10½ to M-13	M-13 and larger

*These are guidelines only. The above reflects the most commonly used gauges and hook sizes for specific yarn categories.

MATERIAL SOURCES

If you're interested in using some of the yarns or tools used in this book, please check out the following resources!

6060
www.6060.etsy.com
Online retailer of a unique variety of plastic safety eyes

American Felt & Craft
www.americanfeltandcraft.com
Online retailer of fine wool felts

Cascade Yarn
www.cascadeyarn.com
Wholesaler and distributor of fine yarns

Clover
www.clover-usa.com
Hooks and notions, available at local craft stores

Delta Sobo Craft Glue
www.plaidonline.com
Glue and craft supplies

Fiskars
www.fiskars.com
Scissors and cutting mats, available at local craft stores

Glass Eyes Online
www.glasseyesonline.com
An international source of glass and safety eyes

Hobbs Bonded Fibers
www.hobbsbondedfibers.com
Poly-down fiberfill toy stuffing and black batting, available at local craft stores

METRIC CONVERSIONS

In this book, I've mostly used inch measurements, with anything less than one shown as a fraction.

If you want to convert those to metric measurements, please use the following formulas:

Fractions to Decimals

$1/8$ = .125

$1/4$ = .25

$1/2$ = .5

$5/8$ = .625

$3/4$ = .75

Imperial to Metric Conversion

Multiply inches by 25.4 to get millimeters

Multiply inches by 2.54 to get centimeters

For example, if you wanted to convert $1\frac{1}{8}$ inches to millimeters:

1.125 in. x 25.4 mm = 28.575 mm

PROJECT COLORS

All of the projects in this book were made using Cascade Heritage 150 sock weight yarn in the colors outlined below. Feel free to use your favorite brand of sock weight yarn (available online and through your local yarn shop).

North Pole

Santa: snow (5618), white (5682) real black (5672), camel (5610), red (5607), moss (5612). Felt: egg yolk, black.

Mrs. Claus: snow (5618), white (5682) real black (5672), camel (5610), red (5607), bark (5609).

Reindeer: snow (5618), real black (5672), camel (5610), bark (5609). Felt: poinsettia.

Elf: camel (5610), red (5607), moss (5612), bark (5609). Felt: egg yolk, black.

Stocking: snow (5618), red (5607).

Present: pagoda blue (5703). Felt: peacock.

Christmas Tree: bark (5609), pine (5612), snow (5618), yolk (5691).

Christmas Goodies

Figgy Pudding: snow (5618), bark (5609), moss (5612), camel (5610).

Gingerbread Kids: snow (5618), camel (5610) or bark (5609).

Gingerbread House: white (5682), bark (5609), red (5607), ultramarine green (5699).

Candy Cane: white (5682), red (5607).

Hot Chocolate: white (5682), red (5607), bark (5609).

Fun in the Snow

Snowflake: pagoda blue (5703), anis (5630), white (5682).

Snowman: white (5682), real black (5672), cinnamon (5640), bark (5609). Felt: beet.

Polar Bear: white (5682), black (5672). Felt: cabbage.

Penguin: white (5682), real black (5672), anis (5630), cinnamon (5640). Felt: forget me not.

Baby's First Christmas

Sleepy Sheep: snow (5618), dark denim (5702).

Mitten Mouse: snow (5618), silver (5697), cotton candy (5628), real black (5672).

Mitten without mouse: snow (5618), charcoal (5631).

Baby Shoes: trellis (5701).

Teddy Heart: camel (5610), snow (5618), radiant orchid (5695), real black (5672).

Woodland Friends

Owl: bark (5609), camel (5610), yolk (5691). Felt: mud puddle, cabbage.

Fox: snow (5618), cinnamon (5640), real black (5672). Felt: cilantro.

Moose: snow (5618), real black (5672), camel (5610), bark (5609). Felt: pine.

Nativity

Christmas Star: white (5682), anis (5630), denim (5604).

Angel: snow (5618), real black (5672), camel (5610), white (5682), yolk (5691), bark (5609).

Baby in the Manger: camel (5610), snow (5618), bark (5609), lemon (5644), yolk (5691).

Mary: camel (5610), anis (5630), pagoda blue (5703), bark (5609).

Joseph: camel (5610), bark (5609), burgundy (5606), atlantic deep (5700). Felt: ivory.

Shepherd and Kings:

  Skin colors: camel (5610), bark (5609).

  Robe colors: ultramarine green (5699), red (5607), dark plum (5632), bark (5609), yolk (5691). Felt: buttercream.

  Head cover colors: snow (5618), yolk (5691), ultramarine green (5699), red (5607), dark plum (5632), bark (5609).

  Hair colors: real black (5672), snow (5618), charcoal (5631).

Camel: camel (5610), real black (5672), bark (5609). Felt: sunshine, pine, egg yolk.

Donkey: snow (5618), real black (5672), silver (5697). Felts: forget me not, hot chocolate.

ABOUT THE AUTHOR

Megan Kreiner grew up on Long Island, New York in a household where art and art projects were a daily part of life. Coming from a long line of knitters and crocheters, Megan learned the craft at an early age from her grandmother, her aunt, and her mother. As of 2012, her MK Crochet and MK Knits pattern lines have been published and featured in numerous books and various crochet and knitting magazines.

A graduate with a fine arts degree in computer graphics and animation from the University of Massachusetts, Amherst, Megan is pursuing a career in the feature animation industry in Los Angeles and currently works as an animator at DreamWorks Animation.

Megan lives in Altadena, California with her husband, Michael, and their children, James and Emily. View her work at MKCrochet.com.

mk crochet ®

ACKNOWLEDGMENTS

Thank you to Matthew and Paul at Spring House Press for keeping me busy and out of trouble by giving me the chance to put this book together.

Thank you to Cascade yarns for being so speedy and generous with their material donations for this book and to American Felt & Craft for spoiling me with a generous stack of felt to play with.

And, finally, thank you to my husband who allowed me to construct a storage area just for yarn in our new office (Merry Christmas to me!) and to my children who have been patiently waiting for months for me to finish this book so I can go back to making crochet toys just for them!

INDEX

*Italicized text indicates a project

PROJECT INDEX BY DIFFICULTY

MORE GREAT BOOKS *from*
SPRING HOUSE PRESS

Crochet Baskets
ISBN: 978-1-940611-61-7
List Price: $22.95 * 96 Pages

Fabulous Fat Quarter Aprons
ISBN: 978-1-940611-39-6
List Price: $12.99 * 56 Pages

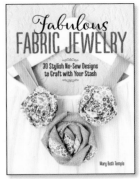

Fabulous Fabric Jewelry
ISBN: 978-1-940611-66-2
List Price: $12.99 * 56 Pages

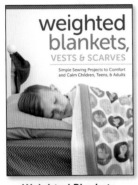

**Weighted Blankets,
Vests & Scarves**
ISBN: 978-1940611-46-4
List Price: $12.99 * 48 Pages

The Natural Beauty Solution
ISBN: 978-1-940611-18-1
List Price: $19.95 * 128 Pages

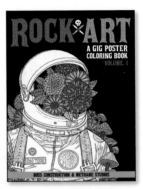

**Rock Art:
A Gig Poster Coloring Book**
ISBN: 978-1940611-42-6
List Price: $12.99 * 80 Pages

**Monkey Business:
An Adult Coloring Book**
ISBN: 978-1940611-43-3
List Price: $9.99 * 96 Pages

**The Wise Owl:
An Adult Coloring Book**
ISBN: 978-1940611-49-5
List Price: $9.99 * 96 Pages

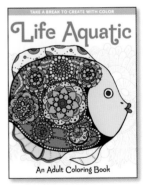

**Life Aquatic:
An Adult Coloring Book**
ISBN: 978-1940611-51-8
List Price: $9.99 * 96 Pages

SPRING HOUSE PRESS

Look for these Spring House Press titles at your favorite bookstore, specialty retailer, or visit *www.springhousepress.com.*
For more information about Spring House Press, call 717-208-3739 or email us at *info@springhousepress.com.*